Richard Byrne was born in  in Manchester, and later stud Economics and Bedford Col wanted to be a lawyer or a characteristic logic into the probation service and remains fascinated by the contrast between real-life and fictional crime. He lives in Manchester with his partner and two children – a household of book and museum addicts.

Richard Byrne

———

PRISONS AND PUNISHMENTS OF LONDON

———

Grafton
An Imprint of HarperCollins*Publishers*

Grafton
An Imprint of HarperCollins*Publishers*
77–85 Fulham Palace Road,
Hammersmith, London W6 8JB

Published by Grafton 1992
9 8 7 6 5 4 3 2 1

First published in Great Britain by
Harrap Books Ltd 1989

ISBN 0 586 21036 9

Set in Bembo

Printed in Great Britain by
HarperCollinsManufacturing Glasgow

ACKNOWLEDGEMENTS

My thanks go to Brian Phythian, Sara Wheeler, Andrew Lownie, R. Harrington, Susanne McDadd and Ian Hyde for the parts they have played in the making of this book. The interest and encouragement of colleagues throughout the staff of Wandsworth Prison kept the idea alive, and the assistance of a large number of librarians and archivists across London made the task feasible. My thanks to all.

PICTURE CREDITS

TABLE OF CONTENTS

INTRODUCTION

The oldest of London's prisons receives more visitors each year than any other building in Britain. Passengers on the Central Line pass beneath the spot at Marble Arch at which 60,000 people were put to death. Men awaiting trial at London courts sit in a prison founded before Victoria came to the throne. There has never been a city with more prisons than London, and probably none whose courts have sent so many to public torment and execution.

For some years I worked in the probation team of Wandsworth Prison, and although it was built more than one hundred years ago the prison is very little changed. Its hundreds of cells have received prisoners each day since before the Crimean War in buildings so little altered that I was easily able to find the windows of our offices in engraved pictures printed in 1862. With a high wall to protect against the sight and sound of life in the 1980s, there is a sense of being in touch not only with the earliest years but with all the history of the prison.

That sense of continuity has provided the motive and the reward as this book was researched and written. I am not a historian, but I am inquisitive about the past, and the story of London's prisons helped me to understand the growth of London. What proved remarkable about prisons was that not only the buildings, but the day-to-day life within them, were described so fully in the records, and how easy it became to imagine scenes and events of the past.

This is a book about the past, and offers only the briefest account of prisons beyond the end of the Second World War. We are in the midst of yet another period of debate about the purpose and utility of imprisonment, and there is great controversy about conditions and events in London's prisons. Although this book may help the reader to perceive how problems have arisen, evidence and comment on the present crisis have been excluded: tomorrow's newspaper will be a much better guide.

THE PRAISE AND VIRTUE OF A JAIL AND JAILERS

In London, and within a mile I ween
There are of jails or prisons full eighteen,
and sixty whipping-posts, and stocks and cages,
Where sin with shame and sorrow hath due wages.
For though the Tower be a castle royal,
Yet there's a prison in't for men disloyal . . .
At last it is a prison unto those
That do their sovereign or his laws oppose.
The Gatehouse for a prison was ordained
When in this land the third King Edward reigned:
Good lodging-rooms and diet it affords . . .
Sich Richard's reign the First the Fleet hath been
A prison, as upon records is seen,
For lodgings, and for bowling, there's large space . . .
Old Newgate I perceive a thievish den,
But yet there's lodging for good honest men . . .
. . . No jail for thieves, though some perhaps as bad,
that break in policy, may there be had.
The Counter in the Poultry is so old
That it in history is not enrolled.
And Wood Street Counter's age we may derive
Since Anno Fifteen Hundred Fifty Five . . .
Bridewell unto my memory comes next,

Where idleness and lechery is vext:
. . . for vagabonds and runagates,
For whores and idle knaves and suchlike mates,
'Tis little better than a jail to those.
Where they chop chalk for meat and drink and
blows . . .
Five jails or prisons are in Southwark placed,
The Counter (once St Margaret's Church defaced),
The Marshalsea, the King's Bench and White Lyon,
Where some like Tantalus or like Ixion
The pinching pain of hunger feel . . .
And some do willingly make their abode
Because they cannot live so well abroad.
Then there's the Clink, where handsome lodgings
be . . .
Cross but the Thames unto St Katherine's then,
There is another hole or den for men
Another in East Smithfield little better,
Will serve to hold the thief or paltry debtor.
The near Three Cranes a jail for heretics,
For Brownists, Familists, and Schismatics.
Lord Wentworth's jail within Whitechapel stands,
And Finsbury, God bless me from their hands!
These eighteen jails so near the City bounded
Are founded and maintained by men confounded:
As one man's meat may be another's bane,
The keeper's full springs from the prisoner's wane.

John Taylor, the Waterman Poet (1623)

THE TOWER

INTRODUCTION

The Tower is the most famous showplace in Britain, and the most deceptive. The millions who visit each year perceive the buildings and exhibits, and are told some of the more exciting tales from its history, but two important truths are lost.

First, the Tower has until recently been a bustling place, in which hundreds lived and followed their trades. There has always been a garrison of troops; in the past there were shipwrights; there were metal-workers manufacturing and maintaining arms and armour; factory hands, supervisors and managers of the Royal Mint; all the servants of the largest household in the land; specialists from astronomers to zoo-keepers. The roadways and spaces of the Tower must always have been crowded, the air full of the sound of men pushing, dragging, hammering, marching, building and demolishing, shouting commands and warnings.

The second is that although its defences have been obsolete since the development of heavy cannon, and no monarch has maintained a court within the Tower for centuries, the Tower has never been decommissioned, never given up its role as a military headquarters, and as the principal state prison of the realm.

Although not deliberately misleading, the guides'

accounts of imprisonment in the Tower dwell upon the individuals – usually royal, or at least noble – and their detention at the mercy of the monarch, but say nothing of the vast majority of the Tower's captives. These were the hundreds who did not come with a retinue of servants to take a suite of comfortable rooms. These were the oppressed Jews of thirteenth-century London; prisoners taken in wars against France, Spain, the United States, the Netherlands and Germany; rebel and traitorous English, resistant Welsh, Irish and Scots; military mutineers; worldly monks who stole royal treasures; religious laymen in theological conflict with the Crown. All these came in their closely-guarded groups, to find a sleeping-space where they could, for the days or years of waiting for ransom, clemency or death.

This must be a very limited account of the Tower and its prisoners. The briefest record of the well-remembered notables would be too long, and too little evidence has survived for us to know about the crude captivity of those thousands of others – their fates, even their names, are lost.

* * *

For its early centuries, the story of the Tower was of its expansion and, once its present outer boundaries had been reached at the end of the thirteenth century, of crowded development, of adaptation and renewal.

After his defeat of Harold in 1066, William the Conqueror did not immediately seize the capital. His plan was to intimidate, then to reach a settlement with some of the divided factions in England, and he led his army on a wildly destructive, skirmishing campaign which laid waste to Southwark before turning away to cut through Surrey, north Hampshire and Berkshire. London was ringed by the devastated path of his line of march – 'devils had come through the land with fire and sword and havoc of war'. It worked, and Saxons cheered their new king on the day of his coronation at Westminster Abbey.

It is a measure of William's nervousness about the untested strength of London opposition that the cheering Saxons were mistaken for a hostile mob, and attacked by William's guard. From his suspicion came the Tower – on land just outside the City; and, controlling movement up the river, William swiftly built a stockaded strongpoint, which was replaced twenty years later by the keep now known as the White Tower. This distinctive square fort was the first substantial castle in England, a powerful demonstration of strength and superior military technology which would overawe the City. We think of the Tower as perfectly British, but it was raised to a Norman design, using Norman skill, even Norman stone.

From this castle William imposed a severe colonial rule. He brought a new system of justice which served him well; he abolished the death penalty, but mutilated, blinded and castrated offenders and resisters – his opponents gained no posthumous glory, but were left as living, helpless advertisements for William's power. This was a calculated ferocity: England was a colony to be subdued as quickly as possible to allow William to return to his more important business in the politics of France. On his death, the kingdom of England went to his second son, the eldest taking the superior title of Duke of Normandy.

Captives must have been taken into the Tower in the Conqueror's reign, but it was William II who committed the first prisoner whom we are able to identify, who was also the first recorded escaper. This was Ranulf Flambard, Bishop of Durham, who had been a minister to the King, but refused to accept a lay court's jurisdiction over his bishopric, and was therefore detained. His captivity must have been comfortable; he was able to keep his servants, and to have provisions and wine brought to him. He used drink to dull his guards, and on 2 February 1106 he climbed down a rope that had been smuggled to him with the casks.

Flambard was held high in the original tower; the most recent prisoners were imprisoned in the outer wall, and we can find a sequence in the expansion of the fortress which reflects the Tower's history as a prison.

The White Tower
The first keep stood within a bailey, an area bounded by a wall which provided the first line of defence. In the late twelfth century a 'gaol' was built within this area, a small lock-up, a petty place of detention for the garrison and the surrounding community. This would have been quite distinct from the chambers used for prominent prisoners, and it disappeared in later building works.

In the mid-thirteenth century, again with the intent of making the keep more impressive, it was painted with coats of whitewash, thus giving it the name which has survived. At about that time it received captives taken in the campaigns to subdue the Scots and the Welsh, among them the unfortunate Gruffydd, who was in 1244 one of the first recorded escapers to try knotting together sheets to make a rope. Technique or material must have been defective – the rope parted, and Gruffydd fell to his death.

In the thirteenth century the Tower was both a place of sanctuary and the scene of atrocious oppression for London's Jews. The Jewish quarter by Cheapside – marked by today's Old Jewry street name – fell within the liberties of the Tower, that area governed by the Constable of the Tower. One of the disputes between the City and the King was the favour which the Constable was said to show Jews in his administration. In fact, because the Jews were taxed exorbitantly, any preference shown was probably preservation of royal revenues rather than protection from anti-Semitism. The entire Jewish community was twice taken within the Tower for safety, but there were also mass detentions of Jews who were in effect held to ransom against payment of enormous demands for cash. By 1278 the King had less need of the Jews' financial support, and in an attempt to gain popularity Edward I imprisoned 600 Jews on false charges of coin-clipping; 260 were executed and most of the remainder died of ill-treatment and neglect, probably in the lowest levels of the White Tower.

In the upper stories very different accommodation was available: King John II of France, who had been captured at Poitiers in 1356, spent three years in luxurious confinement with a full entourage while the money was raised for his ransom.

The Inner Ward

In the thirteenth century the fortifications were extended and strengthened. Two strong outer walls were built, creating the Inner and Outer Wards and making of the whole a mighty modern fortress. Along the inner wall there were now more than a dozen towers, and at the entrance, and along the river frontage, six new towers gave greater protection and accommodation. On the land within this larger castle a piecemeal development provided houses, stores, workshops and barracks for the household and its garrison.

Each of the towers served as a prison at some time, and our names for two of them derive from the family names of the most prominent inmates: Thomas Beauchamp was held in one of the western towers, and Robert Devereux, Earl of Essex, was held in the tower immediately to the north.

As well as the towers, the surrounding houses held prisoners. The Lieutenant's House at the entrance, close by the Bell Tower, was Lady Jane Grey's last lodging. From a window she saw her husband being led from the Beauchamp Tower (where his carving of the name IANE can still be seen) to execution on Tower Hill, and later his body returning on a cart, before her own beheading on Tower Green. One month later Elizabeth Tudor was brought to the Bell Tower, but her health was affected and she was permitted freedom to walk in the Lieutenant's garden and along the stretch of rampart between the Bell and Beauchamp Towers. She had been suspected of taking part in the plots against Mary, but was released after three months when exonerated, surviving to become Queen three years later.

Henry VIII, father to both Mary and Elizabeth, had been the last monarch to use the Tower as a palace, before abandoning it for Whitehall. With his departure, the workshops, chandlery and stores could grow, and the chambers vacated by the court could be used to take more captives. In the words of the official history 'this subsidiary and occasional use became paramount, scarcely a tower or chamber without its prisoner'.

The entanglement of politics and religion in the Tudor and Stuart years brought to the Tower clergy of low and high degree, Protestant and Catholic. Cranmer, Ridley, Latimer and Laud all spent time in the Bloody – or Garden – Tower, while Henry Walpole and many Jesuits were held in the Salt Tower. Failure to follow the religious lead of the monarch was always regarded as treason; the punishment for Catholics was commonly the state penalty of hanging, drawing and quartering, while Protestants died as heretics at the stake.

Often prolonged detention in the Tower need not be uncomfortable. Sir Walter Raleigh was imprisoned by

Elizabeth for seducing one of her maids of honour, but lodged with his cousin, then Master of the Ordnance, whose home was in the Brick Tower. Accused of plotting to place Arabella Stuart on the throne, Raleigh was again imprisoned, by James I. Condemned then reprieved, he spent fourteen years in the Bloody Tower. For all the menace in the name, it was here that Raleigh made a home with his wife, son and servants; he was permitted to turn a ramshackle hen-house into a laboratory; when a further son was born, better accommodation was provided; and Raleigh was able to write his *History of the World* for his patron the Prince of Wales. In all, this was an exile from the affairs of the nation rather than imprisonment as we might understand it. Granted release in 1617 to lead a South American quest for gold, Raleigh returned unsuccessful, and was once more committed to the Tower. At first permitted pleasant rooms in the Wardrobe Tower, he was moved to shabbier quarters high in the Brick Tower, before his last journey to Westminster Gatehouse, Old Palace Yard, and the block, an execution cynically ordered despite the reprieve of fifteen years before.

Wars and rebellions brought great numbers of the obscure and lowly to the Tower, and any secure space was used to take the newcomers – storehouses and cellars, even the elephant house in the menagerie – were pressed into service as cells and wards. Distinctions were made between leaders and followers not only in their imprisonment but in death. As the Scottish risings of the eighteenth century were crushed, many captives were brought to London: hundreds rotted to death at Tothill Fields, dozens went to squalid hanging, drawing and quartering at Kennington, but the aristocratic leaders were lodged well in the Tower and allowed a fairly dignified end on Tower Hill. The last of these, Lord Lovat, is said to have taken instruction from one of his gaolers on how to lower himself to the block, practising with his pillow. (Lovat was aged and infirm: the block now on display, being taller than usual, is thought to have been specially made for his beheading.)

The American War of Independence brought sailors as prisoners of war, and a man who was almost certainly the first democratic politician: Henry Laurens, who had presided over the Continental Congress which drew up the American Declaration of Independence, was taken at sea in 1780, and saw out the war in the Tower. On his release and return to the new United States of America he is said to have gained great prestige for having been a prisoner in such a famous prison.

Fear of the ideas of the French Revolution produced in the English ruling class a feverish reaction, very like the anti-Communist panic of the 1940s and 1950s in the United States. Several men were taken to the Tower on charges of 'constructive treason' when they had expressed approval of the Revolution. Beyond a doubt, the French example encouraged many to be more vocal about their substantial grievances, but the authorities made little distinction between, for instance, rioters and those who merely held membership of political societies. The fearful believed that they were vindicated in 1820 when the Cato Street conspirators – 'physical-force radicals' – were captured before they could carry out a plan to assassinate the Cabinet. The eight prisoners were held separately throughout the Tower, with Arthur Thistlewood, the leader, being accorded the status of a room in the Bloody Tower.

The Outer Ward

In the space between the two encircling walls were the industries of the Tower: foundrywork and smithing, ship repair, and in the north-east corner the Royal Mint. In 1812 the Mint was demolished, and replaced by barracks and a military hospital. It was this military establishment which became the prison quarters in the twentieth century. In the outer wall on the western side are casemates, chambers let into the wall itself, and when the Tower was placed under military control in the two world wars these rooms were used as cells. Although I know of no peacetime detention of civilians in this section, there was at least one occasion between the wars when a military prisoner – a young and foolish officer – had allowed himself to be compromised into revealing low-level information.

Within this section there was also a covered small arms range which was used to execute spies convicted by courts martial – eleven in the First World War and just one man in the Second World War. The Tower was not used for long-term detention, but as a military headquarters it received prisoners of war, such as downed airmen and captured U-boat crews, who arrived in London; civilians suspected of disloyalty, and military offenders.

In 1916 Sir Roger Casement was lodged in the Tower accused of seeking German support for Irish nationalism at the time of the Easter Rising in Dublin. After his trial he was hanged at Pentonville.

Rudolf Hess, Hitler's deputy, spent four days in the Tower after he had parachuted into Scotland on his bizarre peace mission. Sentenced to life imprisonment at the Nuremberg war trials, he may, at his death in Spandau in 1987, have been the last of the thousands who had been prisoners in the Tower of London. This can only be a tentative conclusion: if a national crisis demands, the Tower will resume its role as the supreme state prison. The souvenir shop will close, the tables of the riverside café will be packed away, and the gates of the Middle and Byward Towers will once more close behind men and women accused of treachery.

Tower Green

Many prisoners in the Tower were put to death by royal command, the killings being performed stealthily, secretly, and later denied. An alternative was execution on Tower Green – here royal prisoners could be executed with a pretence of legal form, but away from the public eye when speed and privacy were expedient.

However, the first royal execution was hasty and peremptory: Richard III, when Protector to the young Edward V in 1483, invited a group of noblemen who opposed him to dine in the Tower and while they were at table sent in armed men to seize his enemies. One, the Duke of Hastings, was singled out for execution. He was taken out onto the Green where his neck was laid across a length of timber stored for repair work, and he was beheaded.

Henry VIII revived this use of the Green for discreet execution. His Queens Anne Boleyn and Catherine Howard were beheaded here, and courtiers and nobles who incurred his wrath. One more queen was to die here – Lady Jane Grey in 1554 – and the fallen favourite of a queen, the Earl of Essex, in 1601. Perhaps because they were not noble, the last to die on the Green are rarely recalled: three members of Lord Sempill's Regiment (later to become the Black Watch), who were shot in 1743 for their part in a peaceful protest against poor leadership and conditions. They died in front of the chapel where the other Tower Green victims are buried, and lie beneath the path which leads to its door.

St Katherine's

Close by the eastern wall of the Tower is the ward of St Katherine's. A small debtors' prison stood here for many years, although its importance may be gauged by the fact that on two successive visits in the 1780s one investigator could find neither prisoners nor keeper. There was a rumour for a long time that a secret tunnel led from the Tower to this or the other nearby prison in Wellclose Square, and when the area was being rebuilt there was great public interest in the underground workings discovered here. However, these proved to be evidence not of Tudor plotting but of an early attempt to provide a local pedestrian underpass.

Tower Hill

From and without the Tower ditch, west and by north, is the said Tower hill, sometime a large plot of ground, now greatly straitened by incroachments (unlawfully made and suffered) for gardens and houses . . . Upon this hill is always readily prepared, at the charges of the City, a large scaffold and gallows of timber, for the execution of such traitors or transgressors as are delivered out of the Tower, or otherwise, to the sheriffs of London, by writ, there to be executed.

John Stow, *Survey of London,* 1598

After they had built the Tower, the Normans cleared the high ground which overlooked it to deny potential attackers any cover. Lying just outside the City, the land came to be used as a dump for rubbish of all kinds, and during the Black Death clothing and belongings thought to be contaminated were thrown there, to be cleared only after vigorous complaints from the Constable of the Tower.

The Hill's use as a place of execution began not with state ceremonial but with popular outrage. From an encampment on Tower Hill, Wat Tyler's rebels of 1381 seized the Tower and dragged out Simon of Sudbury, Archbishop of Canterbury, and three other captives, and it was on the Hill that they were messily beheaded using a log as a block; Sudbury's head was taken to London Bridge for display.

Six years later Richard II again faced a threat to his throne from a group of powerful disaffected nobles, known as the Lords Appellant, whose demands he could not resist without immediate deposition. The Appellants insisted on the execution of a man who had been Richard's tutor and mentor, Sir Simon Burley. It was on Tower Hill that Burley's head was cut off, and when Richard was powerful enough to take his revenge he commanded that Arundel, one of the offending lords, be put to death on the very spot where Burley had been killed. Tower Hill had now become a royal place of execution, where treachery would be punished.

The site had the practical advantages of being close to the walls of the Tower and in an area easy to control. In 1440 an Essex priest called Richard Wyche was tried and condemned for his Lollard beliefs. However, there was strong sympathy for the man and his creed among the people and it was decided that a journey to Smithfield – the customary place of execution – carried too great a risk of riot and rescue. Wyche was burned at a stake set on Tower Hill instead and disturbance was avoided. The Hill became a place of pilgrimage for Wyche's supporters, who erected a cross and a stone cairn where he had died. A local vicar sold the martyr's ashes (and restocked the spot with fresh ashes when the demand for relics exceeded the supply). To defeat the pilgrims the Constable of the Tower had the Hill ploughed, and he replaced the cairn with a deterrent dungheap.

The first permanent scaffold was erected in the reign of Edward IV, to the fury of the City. Ownership and rights over land near the Tower had been a source of perpetual conflict since the first fortifications, and the City authorities foresaw that City traders would see no profit from the crowds at executions on the Hill. To pacify the City, Edward offered the arrangement which Stow describes, and the condemned would always be handed over to the sheriffs for execution. In this way honour and the demands of business were satisfied.

Through the years of power struggle and conspiracies Tower Hill was the place where traitors – or those who had merely fallen from favour – were put to death, though a strange class distinction came to apply. The low-born would be taken to Tyburn to hang, but nobles would go to the block on the Hill. One seventeenth-century traitor, a knight rather than a peer, seemed likely to betray his fellow-plotters until they contrived that he should go to Tower Hill – vanity satisfied, he kept their secret. In contrast, the solemnity of the occasion was sometimes deliberately destroyed. When Lord Audley, condemned after the Cornish rebellion of 1497, was paraded to the scaffold in paper armour, mockery was used successfully to blow away popular sympathy.

Sir Thomas More, Thomas Cromwell and Archbishop Laud were dispatched with greater dignity, while Strafford – who with Laud had done most to sustain Charles I – was so despised that 100,000 gathered to shout their contempt and watch his head fall.

The last execution by beheading was that of Lord Lovat, long an intriguer in Stuart politics, who was a baleful eighty-year-old when taken after the '45 rebellion. The vast crowd swarmed over specially erected grandstands, and when one stand collapsed, killing twenty people, Lovat was reported to have found the disaster amusing, chuckling 'The mair mischief, the mair sport'.

The very last executions on the Hill were not beheadings, nor were the condemned high-born. In 1780 anti-Catholic feeling led to the Gordon Riots, and three of those convicted for their part in the disturbances – William

McDonald, Charlotte Gardener and Mary Roberts (a one-armed sailor and two prostitutes) – were taken on to Tower Hill to hang.

At the end of the eighteenth century the Hill was much as Stow had described it, with piecemeal and often ramshackle development eating into an untended open space, until in 1797 an Act of Parliament began the process of improvement.

> . . . Great Tower Hill . . . is and for some time past hath been, in a neglected state and the roads and ways over the same are very inconvenient and in bad condition, and it would be to the benefit and advantage . . . if the said Hill were properly paved, lighted, watched, cleansed, watered, improved and kept in repair and all nuisances and annoyances within the same removed and improved.

The execution of Strafford in 1641 was typical of the many stage-managed executions on Tower Hill.

WELLCLOSE SQUARE
(also known as Neptune Street)

To protect the Tower, the area beyond the moat, known as the Liberty of the Tower, was kept clear. It belonged not to the City but to the Crown, and was the subject of many disputes, as buildings or cultivation encroached upon royal land. In 1686 three further areas, formerly monastic land, were added, one of which was known as Wellclose. Independent of the City and Middlesex authorities, the Liberties and their occupants enjoyed various privileges and had their own administration, including a courthouse and prison.

This prison originally stood on Tower Hill, and may have been the 'Cage' shown on a map of 1597 close to the scaffold. It moved later to Wellclose Square: the building there was small and served as a prison, courthouse and tavern. There are records of the ways in which this ordinary town house was fitted out as a prison: the long narrow garden was roofed with lattice to serve as a prison yard, and the walls and ceilings of three nightrooms were lined with heavy timber which was much more resistant to scraping and hammering than brick or lath-and-plaster.

Residents in the Liberties were rarely called upon to pay rates or local taxes, and the area was so small that there can have been very few paying prisoners. Lacking income, the prison was poorly maintained, and a survey in 1792 described it as ruinous. For all that it was a cosmopolitan lock-up: for several years the innkeeper/gaoler was a Swede, and French prisoners taken in the Peninsular War were brought here when overcrowding in the Tower demanded the use of Wellclose Square as an annexe.

Criminal jurisdiction was removed from the Liberties in the nineteenth century and the prison became a lodging-house.

The Site Now
Wellclose Square and Neptune Street have both now been lost under successive City redevelopments, and no trace remains of the prison.

THE CITY

INTRODUCTION

The City is now crowded by day and empty by night. It is a business quarter in which less than 10,000 people have their home, as custodians of the office blocks and public buildings, or within the recent Barbican complex. The population is lower than in Norman times and only a fraction of the numbers reached in the Middle Ages. It is difficult to visualize the City as it was then – overrun by people and livestock, a frantic trading centre compressed within a strong wall.

It was a city of rumour and sharp practice, to which a steady flow of immigrants came. Fortune-seekers honest and criminal, refugees from rural starvation, to risk the casual violence, disease and neglect through which the wealthy rode in pampered ease.

The successful merchants ruled London and guarded its privileges against royal interference. The people they governed were volatile, quick to respond to religious and political movements – from the puritanical zeal of Lollardry to the democratic demands of Chartism.

The City's prisons held criminals, fraudulent traders, debtors, rioters and preachers. Criminals from areas beyond London were brought to the capital for trial and sentence, but on their release commonly stayed to pursue their careers, going to ground in the sanctuaries and the neighbourhoods in which underworld enterprise flourished. Imprisonment does not appear to have carried the stigma which we now attach to it – the bold lawlessness of criminals often made them heroes and the debtor prisoners attracted more sympathy than the creditors who had placed them behind bars. Arrest and imprisonment were arbitrary when there was no reliable system of justice and the prisons were commonly regarded not as the protection which the state gave to honest people but as the authorities' means of oppressing the poor. Gaols became targets for public wrath much as police officers do today.

Not a single prison remains in the City; like the population itself they have moved outward into the suburbs and beyond. The City's merchant cheats are now more likely to be inside-traders on the financial markets than fishmongers giving short measure, and by a fine irony the kind of trickster who once risked transportation to Bermuda now uses the island as an off-shore base for his operations.

What have been lost are not just the public prisons described here, but hundreds of smaller places of detention too small or short-lived to be chronicled. There were debtors' prisons in private houses – sponging-houses where an officer could detain a prisoner (as always, at a fee), instead of taking his captive to the discomfort of a common gaol. There were small lock-ups in which bad-tempered drunks would be left to sober up, or suspicious characters held until the morning.

From the smallest lock-up to the grandest prison, detention and punishment were very public affairs. The men, women and children in the prisons were on view until the middle of the nineteenth century to anyone with an interest in them, or to the casually curious. Some religious prisoners and the highest enemies of the state were hidden away; for the rest imprisonment was not seclusion. Londoners could enter prisons as spectators, to conduct business with prisoners, drink and sport, or to study the wretches who would soon go to the gallows.

LUDGATE

There were three prisons which bore the name Ludgate, on three separate sites, with a history stretching over 500 years. A Roman gate to the City stood above a crossing of the Fleet River, on what is now called Ludgate Hill; it seems to have been built to allow access to an important burial ground in the Fleet Street area. Later tradition claimed that the gate had been built by the mythical King Lud, and from this tale the hill, the gate and the prison gained their names.

The Lud Gate was rebuilt in about 1215 and, as at other gates, the rooms above the entrance came to be used for detention. It was a small prison, used for petty offenders. In 1382 the Court of Aldermen chose to use Newgate for serious criminals and Ludgate for 'debts, trespasses, accounts and contempts', for clergy and for Freemen of the City. (Freedom of the City was principally the right of master craftsmen to work and trade. In time, qualified masters and merchants enjoyed many privileges; they and their families could call on superior education, charitable help in times of need and exemptions from various City restrictions.)

Ludgate inmates, with a high social standing, did not suffer the worst of medieval imprisonment. Citizens complained in 1419 that the prison was too comfortable, and the management too tolerant, the prisoners 'were more willing to keep abode there than to pay their debts', and that the building was becoming a centre of subversion. To

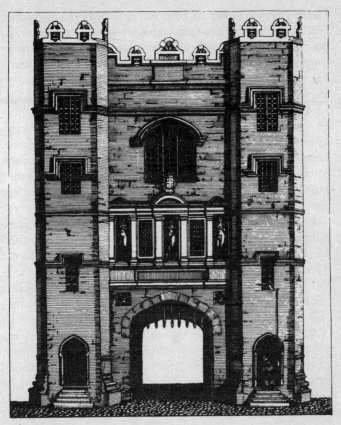

Most of the City gates were to serve as prisons.

stop the rot, the prisoners were transferred to Newgate.
However, Newgate soon became so overcrowded and
unhealthy that within weeks the Ludgate prisoners were
returned to their original gaol.

Dick Whittington rose famously from humble begin-
nings to become Lord Mayor of London, but a comparable
story was that of a Ludgate prisoner, Stephen Forster.

Locked up for debt as a boy, he was begging one day at a grate which gave onto the street when he was noticed by a rich widow. Told that a payment of twenty pounds would release him, she paid the debt and took Forster into her service. He worked loyally and hard, and eventually they married. Prosperous and respectable, he went on to become Mayor in 1454. Ten years later Dame Agnes Forster was widowed again, and she chose to mark their love by improving the lot of prisoners in Ludgate. She paid for a sizeable extension which relieved overcrowding, and provided a chapel and a rooftop exercise area. Further, she insisted that no prisoner should be charged for lodging or for water.

Little of this reform was to last. The building was allowed to fall into decline and the system of payment of fees for every small provision and service was reinstated. The whole building was destroyed in the Great Fire; the prison was rebuilt on the same site, but yet again became the subject of many complaints for its squalor and exploitation of inmates.

When the City walls and gates were demolished in 1760 as obstructions to development and the free flow of traffic, Ludgate's prisoners were removed to a section of the London Workhouse, in Bishopsgate Street, which had been strengthened and prepared for them. This was to have been a temporary lodging, but was still in use until 1794, when a small building and yard next to – and partly encircled by – Giltspur Street Compter was given the Ludgate name. This was probably to retain the prison's special status as the proper place for Freemen, but from being administered separately, this annexe was absorbed into the compter. When the last of the City's debtors' prisons, in Whitecross Street, was built in 1815 the name was revived yet again for the wing in which Freemen were held apart from lesser prisoners.

The Site Now

A plaque on the north side of Ludgate Hill, halfway between Ludgate Circus and St Paul's Cathedral, marks the site of the original gatehouse; the London Workhouse site is lost within the Liverpool Street station. The site of Giltspur Street Compter also bears a plaque.

NEWGATE

Newgate is a dismal prison . . . a place of calamity . . . a habitation of misery, a confused chaos . . . a bottomless pit of violences, a Tower of Babel where all are speakers and no hearers.

*A complete History of the Lives and Robberies
of the Most Notorious Highway-Men* (1719)

Prisoners were held at Newgate from Norman times to the beginning of the twentieth century, in a prison which grew from an adapted lock-up to become the most forbidding and famous prison in the land.

The First Newgate (to 1423)

All the City's gatehouses were originally intended and designed to provide robust defences against attack, but the capital was rarely threatened, and gatehouse accommodation was put to other uses. The authorities would use or let them as stores, and rooms in some of the gates, including Newgate, were regarded as desirable homes for those who could obtain a lease. The City was a crowded, smelly and occasionally dangerous place, and lodgings in the gate offered the convenience of a house in town but at a comfortable remove from the hazards of the crowded lanes and alleys at the centre. The City owned little property which would serve to take prisoners, and all the gatehouses were used at times because their height and solidity offered some security.

Only slowly did Newgate acquire special status. As a lock-up it was certainly overshadowed by its neighbour the Fleet, when it was built around 1130, but in 1187–8 adjoining land was used to extend the gaol; Newgate could then accommodate prisoners from London and beyond, foreign hostages and those deemed a danger to the realm – the most serious of offenders – while minor criminals joined debtors and those held for contempt in Ludgate.

Although – like all prisons – Newgate was technically a royal prison, it was administered by the sheriffs, who in turn sold the ordinary management to keepers. Abuse of the keeper's post was the norm, and for all that they had sworn not to extort money from prisoners beyond an agreed scale of charges, profits were high. Public attention was repeatedly drawn to the misdeeds of keepers, some of whom were removed from their positions, fined and perhaps briefly held in one of the compters, then reinstated to continue their greedy neglect. The decay over which they presided led to escapes and riots, and, worse still, to gaol fever and slow deaths by neglect. The Mayor of London, Dick Whittington, was among the few to show real concern. He admitted that many prisoners perished because of the 'fetid and corrupt atmosphere that is in the heynouse gaol of Newgate', and made a bequest for the rebuilding of Newgate which began in 1423.

Whittington's Newgate (1423–1666)

The immediate nickname of the new prison was 'Whittington's Palace' or 'The Whit'. It was an impressive, five-storey prison, eighty-five feet by fifty, which as a purpose-built prison incorporated some new features. A dining-hall was provided for prisoners; accommodation for those holding the freedom of the City was segregated from that for lower offenders; dark underground rooms provided punishment and extra security for some of the unlucky.

Whatever improvements the new building may have offered, the keepers remained unchanged. In 1449 keeper William Arnold was imprisoned for raping a female prisoner, and wider oppression, blackmail and torture continued despite attempts at inspection. Among the worst abuses was one which offered great profit: ironing the prisoners.

Prisoners were rarely held in separate cells, and to control individual prisoners who were likely to be violent or to try to escape, shackles and fetters would be applied. Since fees were paid by the prisoners both when the irons were put on, and when they were struck off, what could be easier than to apply them to as many prisoners as possible? Further, the heavier the irons, the higher the fees and the greater the incentive to pay. By doubling and trebling the cuffs and fetters a weight of forty pounds was easily reached, and the worst irons were designed to force the prisoner's body into agonizing contortions. The fees were usually paid promptly.

Overcrowding became ever worse as the building was allowed to decay. Expenditure on upkeep and repair would simply have eaten into the keepers' profits, so if a portion of the prison became uninhabitable, the inmates were crammed into the space remaining. This promoted the spread of gaol fever – a form of typhoid which killed many more than the gallows. The Great Plague halted trials, which made the overcrowding even worse. The Great Fire gutted Newgate, at the outermost edge of the destruction, and prisoners were transferred to the Clink while Newgate was yet again rebuilt.

The Third Newgate (1666–1770)

This was still a gatehouse, with towers to either side, and most of the £10,000 cost was frittered on the elaborate decoration of Tuscan pilasters, statues, and worthless battlements. To be a prisoner here was no less arduous than before – 'the sumptuousness of the outside but aggravates the misery of the wretches within' – this was a prison whose stench in warm weather forced neighbouring shops to close, a prison which no doctor would visit, a 'tomb for the living'.

As ever, the wealthy could rent better rooms, eat well, even entertain in style in the Master's Side, if at enormous cost. In the Common Side a hammock or a bare board (perhaps shared) was a costly alternative to lying on the floor 'huddled like slovenly dogs'.

The best lodgings were to be found in the Press Yard. This was the place where those refusing to plead were subjected to *Peine Forte et Dure*, but it was not technically a part of the prison, but of the keeper's residence. If a prisoner had the means, and was not an escape risk, he could live very well here, though it was a frequent complaint that to lodge in Newgate was more expensive than to take a fashionable town house or stay in the best of inns. A prisoner's family would commonly join him, either renting further rooms for the keeper or adding to the overcrowding in the shared wards. Attempts were made to have children lodged in workhouses, where their health could be preserved and they would be safe from the brutality and sexual assaults inevitable in Newgate, yet the surrounding parishes eventually objected to the cost of feeding the extra mouths.

We are so accustomed to thinking of prisons as austere, regimented places that it is hard to picture conditions in Newgate. In a prison designed to hold 150, there were 250 prisoners, together with their families; there were even animals – it was not until 1792 that dogs were banned from the prison, while pigs, pigeons and poultry were not excluded until 1814!

There was an ample supply of cheap alcohol, and drinking and gambling were routine; attempts to ban tobacco and prostitution failed each time. Sexual favours were offered not only for money, but by women awaiting trial who hoped to 'plead their belly' and gain a pardon – if they were charged with a felony, pregnancy was a way of avoiding the rope.

The prison staff was small, and much of the day-to-day running of the prison fell to the prisoners themselves. In 1633 the Court of Aldermen ordered the inmates to hold meetings to elect a warden and wardsmen who would cope with day-to-day difficulties, following the pattern set at Ludgate. This was not a success: the keepers corrupted the scheme, appointing four of their favourites as 'partners' to assist the turnkeys and impose a brutal discipline. In 1724 the partners broke into the wards and stole the charity money that had been collected; some years later they stole the bread ration to sell it, and confiscated all gifts from visitors. Any protests simply provoked further punishment. However, in 1730 the City authorities finally restrained the partners and the prisoners regained some control of their own affairs.

The prisoners' regime was not entirely benign. A custom which extended to all prisons was that of 'garnish', the extraction of money from new prisoners. Since none of the ordinary necessities and comforts were provided by the prison itself, money had to be raised from newcomers to buy candles, coal, soap and other supplies. It was collected on arrival and inability or refusal to pay cash was no use: by force or guile the other prisoners would take clothing or anything else of value.

Prisoners also imposed discipline on each other,

establishing a code of conduct and enforcing it through
tribunals. Since the prisoners' councils had a hand in
distributing charity funds and any rations which arrived,
they had considerable powers.

No work was provided for the prisoners until the
nineteenth century, although debtors always had the right
to follow their trades, and many other prisoners would
make goods for sale to help support themselves.

There was a full-time chaplain, or Ordinary, and
religious services were held which were supposed to
offer spiritual comfort, with severe punishments for those
who disturbed the solemnity of the occasion. In fact, the
Ordinaries were reduced to shouting their sermons – one
complained that prisoners would wander through services
and relieve themselves in a corner of the chapel so that
'there is always an evil smell'.

The services which should have been the most solemn
were the most undignified of all. On the day before they
were due to be hanged prisoners would sit in a railed
enclosure in the centre of the chapel around a coffin,
and hear lengthy preaching about their fate. The public
would watch this spectacle, paying the turnkeys at the
door and creating a carnival atmosphere; and the turnkeys
considered a well-attended service as a satisfactory finale to
the days and weeks of collecting cash from visitors eager
to see the condemned in their hold or cells.

It must not be imagined that the Ordinaries were pious
men struggling to save souls. They were often drawn from
among the least savoury of their calling, and were as ready
to profiteer as anyone else in the prison. Their greatest
opportunity lay in the writing and sale of broadsheets.
Ordinaries had access to condemned prisoners and were
supposed to bring them to contrition and peace of mind,
but these interviews were commonly used to browbeat
the wretched man or woman into giving the chaplain an

exclusive account of the crime, preferably with an affecting confession, which could be sold by the thousand at the execution. Having attended the hanging, the Ordinary might bring out a second edition including an account of the event.

This trade was very lucrative: one Ordinary with an annual salary of £180 died leaving an estate worth £5,000, mostly derived from his pamphlets. If a prisoner refused to co-operate, something could be made up which would serve just as well; plagiarism and conflict over publishing deals were common. The most grotesque example of the value of the trade to the Ordinaries came at Tyburn when a reprieve arrived for a juvenile prisoner which saved him from hanging: the Ordinary had not yet sold all his sheets and, seeing his profits in danger, berated the hangman at length to string the boy up!

In the middle of the eighteenth century it was plain that the City gates caused serious bottlenecks and obstructions to the increased road traffic. For this reason, as much as any intent to improve conditions, plans were drafted and re-drafted for a replacement prison.

The Final Newgate (1770–1901)

The foundation for the new prison was laid in 1770, and the building rose over the next eight years. By 1774 the Sessions House next door was complete, and in that year the gateway itself was demolished. Practical and financial difficulties included the discovery that the Roman ditch beneath the site, to the south of the old gate, was deeper than expected, and foundations had to be taken forty feet down. But, by 1779, the building was complete and the City had a vast and impressive new prison, constructed to a design by George Dance the Younger, a popular and influential architect and City planner.

On 6 June 1780 the Gordon rioters burned Newgate.

Crowds seized the area around the prison, broke in and freed the inmates, then set light to all they could find. Within a few hours, the newest and strongest prison in the realm had become a charred shell. The army was called in to suppress the mob, and prisoners recaptured locally were held in wooden cages hastily erected around St Paul's Cathedral.

The prison was reconstructed with only minor modifications, and was soon nearly as squalid as any previous Newgate, with overcrowding, gaol fever, and venal mismanagement. It may seem extraordinary that after such long consideration, at such expense, and with yet another opportunity to improve the prison offered by the fire, Newgate should so rapidly become once again a penal

The Gordon rioters burn Newgate in 1780.

slum. It was simply rebuilt at the wrong time, for although
there were a few early examples of improved prison design,
there were none in Britain. It is ironic that at the same time
as Dance was supervising the rebuilding of Newgate, from
1785 to 1789, Sir George Onesiphorous Paul was raising
the Gloucester Penitentiary, but none of the lessons and
benefits of this experiment could yet be known.

The keepership of Newgate still only carried a small
salary, which meant that any further income had to be
gained by imposing fees upon prisoners and by avoiding
all possible expense. One keeper, in 1814, refused to
disclose his fee income to an investigating committee,
but offered that only one-third of the operating costs of
Newgate could be met from his salary, and that his final
profit once fees and rents were included came to between
£600 and £1,000 each year.

The City authorities, for their part, often seemed more
concerned to defend Newgate against criticism than to
combat the abuse and neglect.

The public's idea of Newgate's squalor was as important as the reality. Just as detective novels flourished from
the 1920s, and spy fiction took hold on the public's
imagination in the 1960s, so Newgate stories sold by
the cartload in the early 1800s. The serious novels by
Thackeray, Dickens and Harrison Ainsworth were outsold
many times over by cheap reprints from *The Newgate
Calendar*, and eclipsed utterly by the broadsheets of the
trials and executions – more than a million such sheets
were said to have been sold when a murderer called
Thurtell went to the gallows.

The common theme was crime, the heroes were the
criminals, and the climax of the story came when the
hero faced the day of execution and the progress from
Newgate to Tyburn. The reader could enjoy vice and
violence from a safe distance – in the guise of a moral

tale. The most popular figure by far was Jack Sheppard, whose story had been told and re-told since Defoe first saw the drama in his short life; but Claude Duval and Dick Turpin, the highwaymen, and hundreds of lesser villains became the subject of racy and romanticized accounts, in which the imprisonment and execution were always as important as the crimes. There is one modern equivalent – the gangster films with the electric chair to which Jimmy Cagney would walk in the last reel.

Everything about Newgate reinforced the legend. The new building was massive and overbearing, and the public were still able to pay turnkeys to visit and peer into the cells and wards. When the use of Tyburn for executions ended in 1783, burnings and hangings took place until 1868 just outside the high, windowless smoke-blackened walls of Newgate.

There was drama and pathos in the executions, but behind the walls the main cause of distress was over-crowding of extraordinary proportions. The sentence for serious non-capital crimes was transportation, but the loss of the American colonies, and the struggle for control of the seas during the wars with France prevented the sailing of convict ships. As a temporary expedient, unseaworthy vessels, the hulks, took prisoners at their moorings at Portsmouth and Woolwich, but great numbers remained in Newgate after sentence. Wards with inadequate space for thirty or forty people were holding fifty or sixty. The fifteen condemned cells took sixty or seventy at a time. When Newgate was built to take 500 prisoners, the sleeping-space allocated for an inmate was a notional nineteen-inch strip of a planked slope; there were now more than 800 prisoners trying to find a place on those cramped boards.

At the beginning of the nineteenth century there were attempts by Elizabeth Fry and others to reform

Newgate, but no major changes could be made without costly rebuilding. At night, to try to prevent criminal contamination, convicts were separated from prisoners awaiting trial, but this was ineffective. Some improvement came from external events: Whitecross Street Prison relieved Newgate of its debtors, and large-scale transportation was resumed; the number of court sessions was increased to shorten the time spent awaiting trial. Newgate became a depot for prisoners on their way to court or gallows, and when Holloway Prison opened in 1852 the further reduction in numbers allowed some improvement in accommodation. The new belief was that all inmates should be isolated from each other. Grudgingly, and without haste or much apparent enthusiasm for the ideals of the separate system, sections of the prison were converted to single cells.

The Government's national takeover of prisons in 1877 placed Newgate in the hands of the Prison Commissioners – a final victory in a struggle with the City authorities who had resisted supervision or even inspection. Years were then spent in negotiation about the future of the site: the City wanted to extend the Sessions House next door, as well as receive compensation for the loss of the Newgate site. The City was finally obliged to pay £40,000 for the land on which the male wing of Newgate stood, money which the Commissioners used to extend the accommodation at Brixton.

In 1902 Newgate was finally closed. Makeshift corrugated-iron huts in the Press Yard were built to house up to eighty-one prisoners awaiting trial at the Sessions House, and the buildings around them were dismantled. There was an extraordinary auction on the site to dispose of materials and mementoes: eager visitors were led around the prison, even stepping down into the pit of the execution shed, barred only from seeing the punishment cells. Bargain

hunters were able to snap up leg chains and weights for
£4.50, doors for £3.50 to £20.00, and even the prison bell
was sold for £100. An interesting item which revealed the
authorities' nervousness about mob attack was a steel
screen from the main entrance, erected after the Gordon
Riots, 'with sliding shutters in which are six rifle holes
with adjustable covers . . .' As a further reminder, lot 17
was a set of blackened timbers saved from the Newgate
which burned down in 1780, and presumably kept in case
they ever came in useful.

In the same spirit of economy, as much as possible of
the prison's stone facing was kept and used on the Central
Criminal Court – the Old Bailey – which still stands on
the site.

Executions at Newgate

The rebuilding of the 1770s had left a large open area
in front of the prison. This then replaced Tyburn as
the place of public execution, as the procession to the
gallows had become unmanageable – a foul carnival – and
elaborate precautions were always necessary to prevent
rescue attempts. It appeared much simpler to erect a
scaffold directly outside Newgate, and the first execution
was carried out there on 9 December 1783 when ten
people were hanged. An elaborate gallows with a 'drop'
or trapdoor was in use then, but it proved too time-
consuming to erect and dismantle, so for many years a
simple crossbeam was used instead.

The last burning of a condemned woman was outside
Newgate. Burning had been prescribed for women in
cases of treason, where a man would have been hanged
and quartered (regarded as indelicate for women), and for
women who murdered their husbands. Coining was a high
treason, and it was for this that Christian Murphy and her
husband were condemned. He, with seven others, went to

the gallows on 18 March 1789, and when that execution was complete Mrs Murphy was led to a small gibbet, hanged, and then covered with bundles of wood and burned. In the following year this penalty was abolished.

Newgate was also the scene of the last beheading in 1820. The law still provided that traitors should be decapitated and, when five men who had conspired to assassinate the Cabinet as they dined in Grosvenor Square were convicted, this was the sentence of the court. The Cato Street conspiracy had attracted enormous public interest, not least for the bloodthirsty plan to take the heads of Wellington and Castlereagh, and on the day of execution tens of thousands jostled to watch a bizarre performance. The men were led onto a scaffold on which were laid out their coffins. They were hanged, and then, to complete the sentence required by law, each head was severed – after death – by a man in a mask. He used a surgeon's knife instead of the traditional axe, so skilfully that it led to rumours he had in fact been a doctor. Each head in turn was held up to the crowd with the traditional cry: 'This is the head of . . . the traitor!'

But in moving executions from Tyburn the authorities had failed to foresee the dangers of attracting enormous crowds into the restricted area around Newgate Prison. In 1807 a crowd of more than 40,000 had gathered to see the hangings of Owen Haggerty and John Holloway, convicted of the murder of a lavender-maker on an informer's evidence but widely believed to be innocent. A panic began which caused a stampede in which twenty-eight people were killed and nearly seventy seriously injured. On later hanging days barricades were erected in side-streets, although no limit could be imposed on numbers, and the crowd was always very densely packed. Among the onlookers pocket-picking and robbery persisted.

There were no grandstands at Newgate, but rooms overlooking the gallows were let to the wealthy, a special premium being charged for any room from which a clear view was possible on to the drop below the scaffold. Vantage points on roofs cost rather less, and for the groundlings a hanging was one of the great free spectacles of London, a holiday and an occasion to let rip:

I was, purposely, on the spot, from midnight of the night before; and was a near witness of the whole process of the building of the scaffold, the gathering of the crowd, the gradual swelling of the concourse with the coming-on of day, the hanging of the man, the cutting of the body down, and the removal of it into the prison. From the moment of my arrival, when there were but a few score boys in the street, and all those young thieves, and all clustered together behind the barrier nearest the drop – down to the time when I saw the body with its dangling head, being carried on a wooden bier into the gaol – I did not see one token in all the immense crowd; at the windows, in the streets, on the house-tops, anywhere: of any one emotion suitable to the occasion. No sorrow, no salutary terror, no abhorrence, no seriousness; nothing but ribaldry, debauchery, levity, drunkenness and flaunting vice in fifty other shapes . . .

So wrote Charles Dickens in a letter to the *Daily News* in 1846, describing the hanging of Courvoisier six years earlier. The same execution had moved Thackeray to write:

I feel myself ashamed and degraded at the brutal curiosity which took me to that brutal sight . . . It seems to me that I have been abetting an act of frightful wickedness . . . I came away that morning with a disgust for murder, but it was for *the murder I saw done.*

The idea of private executions gained favour – possibly as an alternative to abolishing capital punishment altogether

– and the Capital Punishment Within Prison Act came into effect in May 1868.

In the same month the last public hanging in Britain took place. Michael Barrett, who had planted the bomb at Clerkenwell House of Detention in an attempt to free Fenian prisoners, was hanged before an enormous crowd. The gallows was never brought out again, but was re-erected within a shed in one of the prison's exercise yards, using the beam from the Horsemonger Lane drop. The public was not entirely excluded: for the next twenty years it was still the custom to invite newspaper reporters and special guests of the sheriff. Hanged criminals were buried beneath the passage that led from Sessions House to prison, so that a man condemned quite literally walked on his own grave to and from his trial.

The last hanging in that shed was on 6 May 1902, very shortly before the prison closed, and the apparatus of the scaffold was removed to Pentonville. At the auction of Newgate's contents a bracket which had supported the beam was sold for thirty-five shillings (£1.75).

THE REFORMERS

There are many causes more popular than prison improvement. The squalor behind bars was often little worse than the living conditions of the poor at large; the sick, the orphaned, the victims of famine and disaster, have existed in every age, and with their stronger claim on public sympathy, the smallest attempts to relieve the suffering of prisoners have been derided as offering luxury to the unworthy. For centuries the critics have cried that prisons were becoming so comfortable that, far from deterring criminals, they would encourage crime.

Until late in the eighteenth century it was universally accepted that prisons were best run by private contractors, that the authorities should intervene only in cases of extreme neglect or abuse, and that any distress was yet another regrettable – but unavoidable – fact of life. Much as they might leave money to hospitals, the wealthy would make bequests intended to improve the lot of the poorest prisoners; at Newgate and Ludgate larger legacies made substantial improvement possible, but the effect rarely lasted as much as a single generation.

John Howard   Appointed to a year's term as High Sheriff of Bedfordshire, John Howard was concerned to find that, even after acquittal, prisoners were unable to leave gaol for lack of the discharge fees.

In order to redress the hardship, I applied to the justices of the county for a salary to the jailer in lieu of his fees. The bench were properly affected with the grievance, and willing to grant the relief desired: but they wanted a precedent for charging the county with the expense. I therefore rode into several neighbouring counties in search of one.

That first exploratory journey in 1774 became a remarkable tour of prisons throughout the land, recorded in *The State Of Prisons*, published three years later. This book was notable not just as a plea for change but for the wealth of precise detail it gave of the life of prisoners, from the food they ate to the exact dimensions of the rooms in which they lived, and the space in which they exercised. Howard had himself been a prisoner, a captive of the French some twenty years earlier; this may have helped him to perceive the importance of the prisoner's small world – he was also a landowner who had long tried to give kindly practical expression to his strong Nonconformist Christian beliefs in the attention paid to the conditions of his tenants.

Howard was almost perfectly fitted for the task which he set himself – energetic, persuasive, practical, and very much in tune with his time. He provided evidence and ammunition for those who had felt unease and shame at prison conditions; in each subsequent edition, *The State Of Prisons* was brought up to date with the work of others, such as William Smith, who had surveyed London prisons with a doctor's eye in 1776, and it formed the basis of James Neild's own *State Of The Prisons*, published in 1812, which incorporated the expansions and changes since Howard's visits.

Apart from changing the whole basis of debate and discussion on prisons, Howard was also influential in the law on debt, and indirectly on prison design. He laid down principles of humane separate containment, and made practical suggestions on construction which were followed by a distant cousin, John Haviland, in the building of the Eastern State Penitentiary in Philadelphia, the model for Pentonville and dozens more British prisons.

Howard travelled far beyond Britain to observe and learn about prisons, from the Inquisition in Madrid to Tsarist Russia, and died in the Crimea, of gaol fever, in 1790. In his lifetime he was honoured by liberals and conservatives at home and abroad; penal reform groups around the world bear his name. A less happy legacy was the adoption and distortion of the idea of separation to which Howard himself gave only qualified approval. Later, lesser men applied the principle with a rigidity which Howard's humanity and integrity would have led him to condemn.

Jeremy Bentham   Where Howard was a researcher and a realist, Bentham was a theorist. His contribution to penal thinking was an elaborate scheme for a national penitentiary with a multitude of novel features. It was to be constructed so that all the prisoners would be under constant observation by supervisors stationed at the centre of an enormous circular structure. Since imprisonment was 'a punishment which few or none but individuals of the poorest class are likely to incur', Bentham proposed that prison should be just a little less bearable than the life of the honest poor, so that no one would be tempted to go to prison for its comforts. He believed in isolation and a strict regime, and was sufficiently confident of success to make an offer which might have bankrupted his entire scheme. He proposed to take prisoners at a fee from the state, and not only to give each prisoner a grant on discharge, but to pay the Exchequer if and when an ex-inmate re-offended.

It was Bentham who first purchased the site which Millbank later occupied, but there was no similarity between the building and regime and Bentham's ambitious plan. Millbank was a fiasco, but not the full-blown disaster which Bentham might have created. His circular design – the Panopticon – was adopted in some other countries, and it is reported that prisoners in such a building have a perfect view of staff activity, rather than the other way round.

Elizabeth Fry   No prison reformer has lived so vividly in the public imagination as Elizabeth Fry. It does her no injustice to reflect that her fame was the result both of her deeds, and the perpetual popular astonishment that a *lady* should ever enter a leper colony, refugee camp, or a prison.

Elizabeth Fry was a Quaker, a member of a sect which had been oppressed with imprisonment, beating and execution, and a sect which sets a great value on philanthropy. In 1813 she read a report by a group of American Quakers of their visit to Newgate, where they were 'shocked and sickened . . . by the blaspheming, fighting, dram-drinking, half-naked women'. Fry went to see for herself the filth, desperate overcrowding and hopelessness of women in Newgate, and from this developed a proposal to teach the children held with their mothers. There were objections from the authorities, not least the chaplain, but she overcame them, and although at first she despaired of being able to help the women, Fry formed plans to improve their conditions and assist their reformation. The Association for the Improvement of the Females at Newgate was formed; its first members were Fry and a dozen other strongly religious women. To the prisoners they offered a regime of hard work, discipline and education, all conducted under 'kind superintendence'.

The result was a transformation. Prisoners were now clean, with better food, clothing and bedding, and spent their days in quiet concentration instead of rowdiness. Officials and members of the public remarked on the changes, and despite her own modesty Fry was elevated to the status of an honoured authority. When she visited prisons in other parts of the country where men and women were unsegregated, hers was the voice to which the authorities listened at last – separation was prompt.

The simplicity and goodheartedness of the original scheme seems to have been lost in Fry's later thinking about prison regimes. She was many times called upon as an expert witness, and published her own views and proposals, but over time she came to offer more and more elaborate notions of classification and grading, the emphasis on religious observance became much stronger, and she struggled with ways of staffing prisons with officers who would carry on the firm kindness which her volunteers had shown. Her real legacy lies not in these bureaucratic embellishments, but in the attention which her first work brought to the plight of women prisoners, and her clear demonstration that life behind bars could be orderly, safe and clean.

Elizabeth Fry was the last major amateur reformer. The worthies who took a civic interest in the management of Millbank seem to have had little useful effect, and the changes of later generations were usually the work of public servants, Crown employees with official responsibilities. Life in prison is now much more hidden from public view; the administration of prisons national and complex. Persistent pressure for improvement continues, but this is now the work of organizations rather than outraged individuals.

THE TUN

A tun is a large cask, and this prison, which stood in Cornhill in the Middle Ages, was remarkable for its barrel-like shape – with just a single room on each of two storeys. It was built in 1282 by Henry le Waleis, then mayor, as a lock-up for anyone caught in breach of the City's curfew. Most of those arrested as nightwalkers would have been stray drunks, prostitutes, or their pimps and clients. Other offenders to have been held there included local bakers and millers caught stealing flour, and priests found in illicit intercourse with women.

The law which prescribed detention for incontinent priests gives a glimpse of the medieval use of public disgrace to inflict a punishment as effective as the imprisonment itself: they were to be led 'with minstrels', who presumably gave a loud impromptu account of the offence and its discovery. Other sexual offenders were given similar treatment, and specific routes were prescribed for them: those taken in adultery were to be brought first to Newgate, then through Chepe (Cheapside) to the Tun, while a woman found with a priest would first go to one of the sheriffs' compters.

It must have been well-orchestrated mockery, with the sound of an approaching procession drawing people from their houses to join in the tumult. In the small City of the fourteenth century the miserable captives would be known to many in the crowd, and a secret misdeed would now become quite literally the talk of the town.

The Tun was to have been taken out of use in 1275, but remained a prison until 1401, when it became a cistern in a new supply system which piped water across town from the Tyburn. A simple lock-up cage and stocks were built close by.

ELY PLACE

Like the Savoy and Lambeth Palace, Ely Place was a
grand town house, built in the thirteenth century for the
Bishops of Ely. Tudor monarchs commonly appropriated
church holdings, and in 1576 Elizabeth I made a gift of the
house to Christopher Hatton, her Lord Chancellor and a
current favourite. The bishop tried to resist, and at one
stage managed to retain 'two rooms used as prisons for
those who were arrested or delivered in execution to the
bishop's bailiff' – small compensation.

During the Civil War the house was used both as a
hospital and a prison. Parliament instructed on 3 January
1642:

> The palace was this day ordered to be converted into a prison,
> and John Hunt, sergeant-at-arms, appointed keeper during the
> pleasure of the House. He was at the same time commanded
> to take care that the gardens, trees, chapel, and its windows,
> received no injury.

This house was demolished in 1772, but the Old Mitre
Tavern, originally built as servants' quarters to the main
house, still stands at 1 Ely Place. It is likely – although
unproven – that this was used for detention. The street
remains Crown, rather than City, property, beyond the
authority of the Lord Mayor. Even the police are able to
enter only by invitation.

THE CITY COMPTERS

In the Middle Ages, every powerful person – king, bishop or lord – had judicial power. Each could imprison, each had his personal place of detention within a palace or castle. In London, power was held by elected officials who administered their own justice on all but the very gravest treasons.

In the counties it was common for the administrators of justice to take captives into their own homes for safekeeping, and this probably happened from time to time in London. Lodging in the City gates could be found for others, but the size of the demand exceeded anything makeshift or small, and so for hundreds of years the City had its compters – gaols for petty offenders and debtors, which were more important than the lock-ups, but less significant than the larger prisons.

Each of London's two sheriffs had a compter. A sheriff, or 'Shire Reeve', was a county justice, the local representative of the king's law, but in London always appointed by the City. In 1132 it was granted that London should have two such sheriffs, one for London and one for Middlesex, although in practice both posts were held within the City. Their offices were created before that of the mayor, which followed in 1192; they were both enormously powerful, and occasionally great rivals to each other, jealous of their powers and jurisdiction.

Each sheriff had a large prison, well within the City. They were town houses rather than separate and isolated gaols, and were rarely administered by the sheriffs, but rented out to keepers. The prisons had at least three levels or grades of accommodation, from the comfortable but expensive Knight's Side, through the adequate, mid-priced Master's Side, to a Common Side which was usually a hell on earth.

BREAD STREET COMPTER

This was a very early City gaol. There is no record of its appearance but it was probably a town house like Poultry Compter, the other sheriff's gaol. It must have been quite large: in 1425 when Newgate was being rebuilt using Whittington's bequest, the inmates were temporarily housed in the Bread Street and Poultry compters, and in 1431 Bread Street was able to accommodate all the prisoners from Ludgate in another short-term move.

The keeper of Bread Street in the mid-sixteenth century, Richard Husband, was a 'wilful and headstrong man who dealt hard with the prisoners for his own advantage', and hired servants who were as brutal as himself. Despite many complaints, he refused to change his ways, and in 1550 the mayor sent him to Newgate with instructions that he be kept in irons. He was held for a few days, and then released and reinstated, but was to forfeit a hundred marks if he offended again. Husband not only continued to cheat his prisoners, but developed a further sideline by offering lodging to thieves and strumpets for fourpence a night, so that they could hide from the authorities. Attempts were made to punish him, but he could not be removed from Bread Street as he held a valid title to the building. Stow was a member of one jury which had considered the case, and his comment would serve for any of the prisons bought and sold for profit: 'Note, that gaolers buying their offices will deal hardly with pitiful prisoners.'

Bread Street Compter closed in 1555, and the prisoners were transferred to Wood Street Compter. Having failed to remove the keeper from the gaol, the sheriff may well have chosen to remove the gaol from the keeper.

POULTRY COMPTER

> The Counter in the Poultry is so old
> That it in history is not enrolled.
>
> John Taylor (1623)

Certainly it is difficult to state firmly just when the compter in Poultry was built. It was probably a fourteenth-century foundation, a strengthened town house rather than a specialized, separate building. One sketch map showed it as lying north of Poultry at the rear of a courtyard reached through an alley.

Like Wood Street, this is a prison best remembered for the ripe invective of those who had spent time there . . . Thomas Dekker, who had been a prisoner in 1598, wrote of the sounds of the gaol:

> . . . jailers hoarsely and harshly bawling for prisoners to their bed, and prisoners reviling and cursing jailers for making such a hellish din. Then to hear some in their chambers singing and dancing, being half drunk; others breaking open doors to get more drink to be whole drunk. Some roaring for tobacco; others raging and bidding hell's plague on all tobacco . . .

Of the smells and sights, Ned Ward, the publican poet and author of *The London Spy*, wrote a century later:

> . . . a mixture of scents from mundungus, tobacco, foul feet, dirty sheets, stinking breaths, and unclean carcases . . . far worse than a Southwark ditch, a tanner's yard, or a tallow chandler's melting-room. The ill-looking vermin, with long rusty beards, swaddled up rags, and their heads – some covered with thrum caps and others thrust into the tops of old stockings.

Among the debtors and wayward writers, the compter occasionally held an exotic prisoner such as Dr Lambe, imprisoned in 1628 after he was said to have supplied the

Duke of Buckingham with a love philtre, and charged with 'certaine Evil Diabolicall and Execrable arts called witchcraft'.

Describing in 1801 a prison which was smaller and held fewer people only because it was so decayed, Neild wrote:

> The 36 debtors had 11 wives and 17 children living with them in the prison. They are allowed rugs by the city, but must find their own beds . . . In one of the rooms on the second floor (called the Pump Room), the debtors have the convenience of water. The rooms were out of repair, but the debtors kept their floors clean . . . All the other parts of this close and crowded prison are in so ruinous and insecure a state, that, if it was not shored up in many places, it would tumble down.

One year later the danger was so great that the prisoners were moved temporarily to Giltspur Street while basic repairs were put in hand; this seems to have consisted in no more than pulling down that which was falling down. The prisoners were then sent back, but ten years later demolition followed the removal of the prisoners to Whitecross Street.

The Site Now

On the north side of Poultry, where the compter once stood, is the headquarters of the Midland Bank.

WOOD STREET COMPTER

This was the successor to Bread Street Compter and received its first prisoners in 1555. It rapidly gained notoriety as the scene of ruthless exploitation and heartless neglect. Fennor's account (*see* The Counter's Commonwealth) may seem overstated, but it did no more than echo a petition of some twenty years before:

. . . we the miserable multitude of very poor distressed prisoners, in the Hole of Wood Street Counter, in number fifty poor men or thereabouts, lying upon bare boards, still languishing in great need, cold and misery, who by reason of this dangerous and troublesome time, be almost famished and hunger-starved to death; others very sore sick, and diseased for want of relief and sustenance, by reason of the great number which daily increaseth . . .

The compter was destroyed by the Great Fire of 1666, but was rebuilt on the same site. Neither building was set apart from its neighbours by a yard or wall, but went straight on to the street in the manner of a town house or business premises. This allowed prisoners to beg for cash or food from passers-by.

Wood Street Compter closed in 1897, and its prisoners were moved to the new Giltspur Street Compter.

The Site Now
All traces of the prison have disappeared above ground, but part of the cellars has survived. The underground rooms were long used for wine bottling and storage, but are now owned by a local wine merchant and may be hired for parties and other functions. The entrance to those cellars is down an alleyway off the eastern side of Wood Street, between Cheapside and Gresham Street.

THE COUNTER'S
COMMONWEALTH

**or a voyage made to an infernal island
discovered by many captains, seafaring men,
gentlemen, merchants and other tradesmen.**

In 1616 William Fennor, a poet and performer, was
arrested for a minor assault and taken to Wood Street
Compter. Enraged by the treatment he received
and all he saw about him, he published in the
following year an account of the prison which is
both wonderfully vitriolic, and a valuable eyewitness
account of life behind bars. It is easy to imagine him
committing his observations to memory against the
day when he would have his say.

On fees 'For what extreme extortion is it when
a gentleman is brought in by the watch for some
misdemeanour committed, that he must pay at least
an angell before he be discharged; he must pay
twelvepence for turning the key at the master-side
dore two shillings to the chamberleine, twelvepence
for his garnish for wine, tenpence for his dinner,
whether he stay or no, and when he come to
be discharged at the booke, it will cost at least
three shillings and sixpence more, besides sixpence
for the book-keeper's paines, and sixpence for the
porter . . . And if a gentleman stay there but one
night, he must pay for his garnish sixteene pence,
besides a groate for his lodging, and so much for his
sheetes . . . When a gentleman is upon his discharge,
and hath given satisfaction for his executions, they
must have fees for irons, three halfepence in the
pound, besides the other fees, so that if a man were in

for a thousand or fifteene hundred pound execution, they will if a man is so madde have so many three halfepence.'

On gaolers '. . . men that, having run through their trades as they have their estates, at last are forced to take upon themselves this most base and odious kind of life; which they no sooner have obtained but are as proud of it as a lousy prisoner of a fresh suit, or a beggarly rhymer of twelvepenny dole when he oweth ninepence for ale. They are men that have no quality in them but one, and that is to ask money, and, like lawyers, without their fees they will do nothing. They imitate ravens, kites and crows that feed upon the corruption, stinking garbage, and guts of any carrion . . . so these feed upon the follies and vices of the age . . .'

On prisoners pursuing their trades within the compter '. . . heere you shall see a cobler mending old showes, and singing as merrily as if he were under a stall abroad; not far from him you shall see a tailor sit cross-legged (like a witch) on his cushion . . . you may behold a saddler empanelling all his wits together how to patch this Scotchpadde handsomely, or mend the old gentlewoman's cropper that was almost burst in pieces. You may have a physician here, that for a bottle of sack will undertake to give you as goode a medicine for melancholy as any doctor will for five pounds. Besides, if you desire to be removed before a judge, you shall have a tinker-like attorney not far distant from you, that in stopping up one hole in a broken cause, will make twenty before he hath made an end, and at last will

Wood Street Compter. A plain City building, but a warehouse of squalor and despair.

leave you in prison as bare of money as he himself is of honesty.'

On conditions in The Hole 'In this place a man shall not look about him but some poor soul or other lies groaning and labouring under the burthen of some dangerous disease; the child weeping over his dying father, the mother over her sick child; one friend over another, who can no sooner rise from him, but he is ready to stumble over another in as miserable a plight as him he but newly took his leave of. So that if a man come thither he at first will think himself in some churchyard that hath been fattened with some great plague, for they lie together like so many graves.'

GILTSPUR STREET COMPTER

This small but complex prison was built in 1791 to a design of George Dance the Younger. It held debtors and minor offenders; since overnight prisoners could not be held in the City's watchhouses, they were brought to Giltspur Street, then marched out each morning to a hearing before the Lord Mayor or an alderman.

This was a busy prison, with 6,000 committals each year. Records show that 100 visitors would call each weekday, and twice as many on Sundays.

Intended to hold 203 prisoners, forty or fifty more were often accommodated; of the total, thirty or forty would be debtors. It seems to have had an easygoing regime, with only twenty punishments imposed in a year, and frequent escapes. In a maddening aside to stir our curiosity, the Inspectors of Prisons observed, after citing a couple of weaknesses in Giltspur Street's security, that 'There is another circumstance which renders this prison very insecure but which we do not think it prudent to notice'.

Within Giltspur Street prisoners were divided into four classes: Debtors, Felons, Misdemeanours and Assaults, though few felons were probably held here. The prison was divided into nine distinct yards, and it appears that inmates were shuffled around the prison according to the space available rather than their class. One oddity was that solitary confinement was in cells which overlooked the street, and prisoners placed in them for punishment were able to see and talk to passers-by; when executions were held just a hundred yards away outside Newgate, they could call to the crowd.

Giltspur Street Compter was demolished in 1855, the prisoners having been moved to Whitecross Street.

The Site Now

Giltspur Street meets the junction of Holborn Viaduct, Newgate Street and Old Bailey, just opposite the Central Criminal Court. Close to the junction, opposite St Sepulchre's Church, is a plaque which marks the site of the compter.

WHITECROSS STREET

This was the last of the City's debtors' prisons. At the beginning of the nineteenth century there was concern that Newgate continued to hold debtors alongside criminals, and pressure led by Sir Richard Phillips, sheriff in 1807, resulted in parliamentary permission to build a new prison. However, the local residents were less easily swayed, and there was strong opposition to the plans for a tall surrounding wall, which was considered to be an eyesore; to the destruction of houses which provided an income for a local church, and to the cost of the project.

Nonetheless, building began in 1813, and Newgate's last debtors became the first Whitecross Street prisoners in 1815. Two years later, with the demolition of the Poultry Compter, the number of inmates increased, although it rarely reached the full capacity of 490. The early fears about cost were justified: the building was more expensive than promised, and the cost per prisoner was high. The money had bought a dreary gaol with a degree of security which was never justified by the type of prisoner held:

these were not desperadoes, and the average stay lasted no more than ten days. Links with the past were kept in the names of the prison's divisions: Poultry, Giltspur Street and, as ever, Ludgate for Freemen.

Throughout the prison's existence, its original purpose was fading. Successive changes in the law reduced the numbers of imprisoned debtors, until the effective abolition of imprisonment for this group in 1870.

There was to be a grand finale. The terms of the 1869 Debtors' Act produced a rush of people *wanting* to be committed to prison, since by service just a few days behind bars they would be forever free of their debts. Many seized the opportunity, and Whitecross Street was busier than it had been for decades. At the end, only twenty-seven prisoners remained, who were transferred to Holloway in July 1870.

The Site Now

The site was cleared in 1877, and a railway goods depot was built here. This was destroyed in the Second World War, and the whole district was covered by the modern Barbican development.

ALONG THE FLEET

INTRODUCTION

Peer under the north side of Blackfriars Bridge, and you will see a pair of pipes. This is now the mouth of the Fleet River, and the water dropping into the Thames has made its way down a winding valley from Hampstead Heath and Parliament Hill, via Camden Town and Clerkenwell.

They say that the Fleet is a river which has declined to a brook, to a ditch, to a drain, and it is certainly difficult to imagine that there was once a river navigable for at least half a mile up from those twin culverts. To grasp how the Fleet and its valley have had a place in the development of London and its prisons, brave the traffic and stand on the traffic island at the northern end of Blackfriars Bridge, narrow your eyes, and conjure an image of Farringdon Street as the line of a valley stretching north beyond the bridge of Holborn Viaduct.

You will then see (despite the confusing rooflines) how the ground rises quite steeply to the east, and it was on that lip of the valley that the Romans built their wall. There is a plaque halfway up Ludgate Hill, and it is quite easy to imagine a rampart running from there, just uphill of the street called Old Bailey, to the Newgate plaque on Newgate Street.

The Romans had established a strong defensive line, a

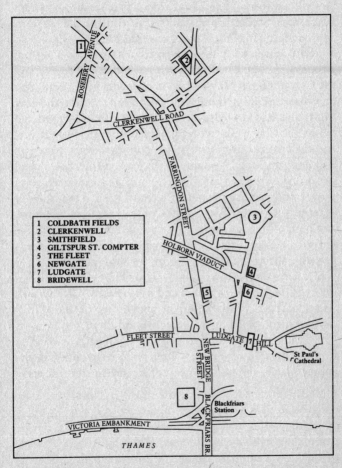

1 COLDBATH FIELDS
2 CLERKENWELL
3 SMITHFIELD
4 GILTSPUR ST. COMPTER
5 THE FLEET
6 NEWGATE
7 LUDGATE
8 BRIDEWELL

Along the Fleet

firm western boundary to their city of Londinium, and when William the Conqueror wanted to dominate London he built a fortress, called Baynard's Castle – roughly where Blackfriars Station now stands – to control the western approach much as the Tower covered the east.

Many cities have housed their prisoners in a central stronghold, but London's castles were at the edges, and the City confined only its minor offenders in the compters at its heart, sending those who were a real threat to the City limits and beyond. The Fleet prison was built beyond and below the City walls, with a moat fed from the Fleet River, and the two major gates overlooking the Fleet – Newgate and Ludgate – were also important gaols. Other gates were occasionally pressed into service, but the second centre of power and development had already been established at Westminster when Edward the Confessor moved his court, and built his Abbey there. The river and the roads from the City to Westminster were to form the axes of London's growth. Bridewell and the Savoy lay along that line.

Crossing this east–west line was the Fleet valley, and this directed development uphill and northwards. Clerkenwell and Coldbath Fields stood at the limits of the City's development, with broad fields around them.

All these prisons formed one side of an early inner ring in the City's development; outer rings were added in the suburbs later, and like the heart of an ancient tree, the early prisons died.

THE FLEET

The Fleet was the first prison in London to be conceived, designed and built as a gaol, and stood on the same site on the eastern bank of the Fleet River, just outside the City walls, for nearly 700 years, from soon after the Norman Conquest to the reign of Queen Victoria.

The first prison, fortified and moated, was an intimidat-
ing strongpoint as well as a place of detention: like the
Tower to the east, it was a symbol of the new dynasty's
power, and the keepership of the Fleet was a royal
appointment. At a time when imprisonment was not
used systematically as a punishment, the Fleet will have held
curfew-breaking drunks alongside the king's political foes.

Over the years the major London prisons acquired their
distinctive characters both through custom and tradition,
and also from the courts which they served. The Tower,
for example, tended to take fewer common criminals
and more major political prisoners, and thus became a
state prison; the Clink was used for religious offenders,
while the Marshalsea and the Fleet were used in the
administration of royal justice. The Fleet specialized
further in holding those who owed money to the Crown,
and those committed by the King's Council and the Court
of Chancery. Many such prisoners had not offended under
common law or statute, but had merely affronted or
embarrassed the king, and were deemed to be in contempt
of one of his courts.

The keepers were royal appointees, but were far from
being civil servants: running a prison was a profitable
business and became a property which might be inherited,
bought and sold. A single family retained the office for
more than 400 years: the Levelands had a manorial title
in Kent to which the keepership was attached, and two
of the earliest keepers were women – widows of keepers
who inherited and ran the family business.

The first prison decayed, and needed to be rebuilt by
the reign of Edward III, and again after being razed
by Wat Tyler's rebels in 1381. The moat was filled in
as a public nuisance, having been 'choked up by filth
and latrines built thereon', and so clogged with offal
from nearby slaughterers it was said that a man might

walk across. The operation of the Fleet was close to a modern pyramid-selling operation: every officeholder paid for his position (a lowly portership cost £20 in 1558), and payment was made upwards at every level, the value of the keepership when sold on the open market in 1559 reaching £8,000. At the bottom were the unwilling paying customers, held for heresy, crime, debt or incurring the royal displeasure, who paid for every small service.

Alongside the countless anonymous poor were notables whose offences and fates are known: John Donne was imprisoned for marrying without the consent of his bride's father; prisoners of conscience included Bishop Hooper who went from the Fleet to die at the stake in Gloucester; Prynne and Lilburne, Puritan anti-Royalists, were punished for pamphleteering by imprisonment, the pillory and mutilation. A luckier prisoner was the dramatist William Wycherley who was committed to the Fleet when he fell upon hard times, but released by order of King James, who mistakenly believed that a character in one of Wycherley's plays was a flattering portrayal of himself.

The prison was destroyed in the Great Fire, but rebuilt much as before, and the prisoners returned from temporary lodging in Lambeth. Behind a narrow yard stood a long building with a small additional wing at each end; there were other yards, including a large rackets ground used by both prisoners and public and a smaller area called 'The Painted Ground' when a prisoner covered a wall with murals of men-of-war and other elaborate designs.

The buildings had four upper storeys and a cellar, called 'Bartholomew Fair', in which the poorest lodged; better-off prisoners might inhabit bare wards, or, for a little more expense, cubicles around the ward walls; while on the Master's Side were spacious comfortable rooms. The prison had a coffee-room and a tap-room which provided income for the management, and even the chapel was turned to profitable use (*see* Fleet Marriages).

A full account of the misery and squalor of the Fleet reached the public in 1691 in Moses Pitt's *The Cry Of The Oppressed*, written when Pitt was in the Fleet, and published at his own expense despite obstruction from the authorities. Details of the filth, disease, torture and extortion were set out in support of a petition to Parliament for relief of poor debtors. Among the abuses he condemned was an oddity of the law unique to the Fleet, by which a creditor had the right to a writ of habeas corpus which would cause a debtor to be transferred to the Fleet from any other prison. The Fleet was the most expensive prison in the country, and the staff found it worthwhile to approach creditors with inducements to take out writs and provide them with fresh inmates to milk.

Although there was great interest in Pitt's story, no important reforms resulted. Thirty years later Thomas Bambridge, keeper of the Fleet, was accused of 'great extortions, and the highest crimes and misdemeanours in the execution of his said office' by a parliamentary inquiry, because he had 'arbitrarily and unlawfully loaded with irons, put into dungeons, and destroyed prisoners for debt', and it emerged that not only had Bambridge taken money to permit escapes, but had even provided a special exit door for the purpose. The keeper was sent for trial, but acquitted; popular feeling ran so high that an Act was passed to dismiss him, and new rules were framed for future keepers.

The Fleet was destroyed by fire yet again in the Gordon Riots, but with an odd courtesy the rioters sent a note to the prison announcing their attack. One rioter was shot on the roof of the prison while taunting and hurling tiles at the soldiers trying to restore order, but there seem to have been no other casualties.

Again rebuilt, the new prison had the number 9 above
its entrance gate, and the polite custom when writing to an
imprisoned debtor was to give as the address 'No 9 Fleet
Market'. But euphemism could not disguise the fact that
conditions were still appalling. John Howard visited the
prison before and after the fire and wrote damningly on
both occasions. His concern was for the poorest and most
wretched, for as ever the life of the well-heeled could be
perfectly bearable. It may seem contradictory for debtors
to be able to afford the regime, but within the prison
and the surrounding area (*see* Liberty of the Fleet) were
many who were in fact sheltering from creditors, having
recklessly or fraudulently run up debts. For them, and for
their friends, there were sports, entertainments and bars
which were open to casual visitors as well as prisoners.
In 1820 a serving prisoner called Robert Mackay became
world rackets champion, beating all comers.

An inquiry into conditions in the Fleet in 1819 found
240 to 250 inmates within the prison, and a further
sixty or seventy in the Rules. Thirty-nine wives and
fifty-four children lived within the prison; all staff still
received income only from prisoners' fees, and alcohol and
prostitutes were admitted without serious restriction. At a
time when penal reform was being so widely discussed, the
Commission's report was strangely indulgent, and made
few recommendations beyond the closure of the tap-room
and coffee-room during Sunday chapel services. Their
researches had also included the Marshalsea and King's
Bench, but as with the other old debtors' prisons, they
all became redundant with changes in the law on debt. In
1842 the three were amalgamated; all the prisoners were
to be held in the King's Bench (renamed Queen's Bench
for Victoria), and the Marshalsea and Fleet were closed.

The Fleet finally closed after more than 700 years
of operation. The site remained derelict until the

Congregational Memorial Hall was built there, dedicated to the memory of the dissenting ministers who had been ejected from the Church by the Act of Uniformity in 1662 – many of those ministers having been imprisoned in the Fleet. The hall, in its turn, found a place in history as the birthplace of the Labour Party, founded at the Trades Union Congress of 1900. From this building the General Strike of 1926 was organized.

The Site Now

On the eastern side of Farringdon Street, about halfway between Ludgate Circus and the bridge of Holborn Viaduct, stands Caroone House, an office building which still contains a Memorial Hall at the rear. There is a further historical connection in the name of the office: when the prison was evacuated during the Great Fire, the prisoners were taken to the home of the Dutch Ambassador in Lambeth, a mansion called Caroone House.

LIBERTY OF THE FLEET

From the time of Richard II prisoners in the Fleet were permitted out for the day if they posted bail or were accompanied (at a fee, of course) by a tipstaff. In time this privilege was extended so that a prisoner might take lodging in houses close to the prison if he paid the keeper to compensate him for the loss of earnings, and either posted bail or lodged money to cover a proportion of his debts. Simple bribery would also do nicely. The area in which this privilege could be exercised was known as the Liberty, or Rules of the Fleet; only prisoners in the King's Bench could wander so widely. In time the Liberty grew to a district a mile-and-a-half across.

Just as they could work in their trades and professions within the prison, so prisoners prospered in the Rules. Clergymen made money by conducting Fleet Marriages, and the Fleet's closeness to the centre of the publishing trade around St Paul's (and perhaps the tendency of hacks to drift into drink, debt and misdemeanour) led to a considerable writing, editing and publishing industry.

FLEET MARRIAGES

At the beginning of the seventeenth century a new opportunity for profit was seized at the Fleet prison. Couples wishing to marry in haste or secrecy had been able to use a chapel within the White Tower of the Tower; when this was stopped, the ministers of two local parishes continued the trade. One of these churchmen, having been suspended, transferred his business to the Fleet Chapel. Clergymen detained in the prison expanded the trade, but the fame of the practice spread so that informers would keep an eye on the couples arriving in hope of reward. The solution was to move out of the prison into the Liberty of the prison, since at that time the law did not require marriages to be conducted on authorized premises. Ministers, and those purporting to be ministers, set up shop in taverns and houses throughout the neighbourhood, kept registers for a show of legitimacy, and employed touts to bring in custom. Turnkeys and other prison staff were prominent in the trade.

Tens of thousands of couples went through these ceremonies, often quite drunk and after the briefest acquaintance with their brides or grooms: when the fleet was in port, there might be two or three hundred sailors' marriages within the week. The scale, showmanship and shabbiness of the trade makes the storefront wedding chapels of Reno look like discreet models of decorum.

Despite protests that without such a cheap alternative the poor might live in sin rather than wed, the Marriage Act of 1753 put an end to Fleet weddings, and probably set future adventurers and heiresses on the road to Gretna Green.

BRIDEWELL

Like the Clink, and Borstal, Bridewell Palace has given its name to penal history. Prisons and police stations throughout the country have carried its name – a fine irony for what was once a magnificent royal palace.

Bridewell was built in 1515–20 for Henry VIII, on a vast site alongside the western bank of the Fleet River, reaching up from the Thames to the present Fleet Street, a rambling spacious complex built around three large courtyards. It came to be used as lodging and an embassy for foreign monarchs and dignitaries: Charles V, Holy Roman Emperor, was entertained here in 1522, and from 1531 to 1539 the French Ambassador took a lease on the palace.

Its use was changed in the sixteenth century, when London was expanding very rapidly, but could not provide for all the displaced poor people who arrived in tens of thousands from across the country. Most were honest, many begged until they could find work, but among them were organized bands of robbers and rowdies. Concern for the poor was mixed with fear of the threat to public order. In 1550 Edward VI took to heart a sermon on the plight of the needy, and the duty of those who had wealth and privilege to offer alms, and supported the City in a petition to the Privy Council calling for Bridewell to be given over to the relief of the poor.

Simple charity became joined and confused with an attempt to remove the threat of idleness and lawlessness. The idea took over that enforced labour and punishment would reform the work-shy, the drunkard and the petty thief, and from the beginning Bridewell was run not only as a refuge but as a workhouse. The very size of the buildings recommended it for the purpose:

> . . . And unto this shall be brought the sturdy and idle: and likewise such prisoners as are quite at the sessions, that they may be set to labour. And for that number will be great the place where they shall be exercised must also be great.

The pattern was set at Bridewell for future labour in prisons, and for the vast Victorian workhouses.

By 1556 the first prisoners had been received, and put to a wide variety of trades. Some of the work had an element of skill, such as carding and spinning, and the manufacture of nails, but there was cruder work, for those who were to be punished as well as detained, such as cleaning the sewers in gangs, or beating hemp in wards. Treadmills were installed and even an ingenious hand-and-foot mill invented to make sure that anyone who had lost a limb should not be excused labour.

HOUSES OF CORRECTION

Monarchs and governments have always feared the wandering unemployed. People on the move had no masters, and would be at best a burden, at worst a serious threat to any community in their path. We hear echoes of those old dreads in the rejection of jobless young men looking for work in seaside towns – sanctions must be imposed to drive them back whence they came, or at least to keep them on the move.

Today most of these travellers will commit no offence more dreadful than sitting in a bus shelter to drink lager straight from the can, under the watchful eye of the police. They can never be the threat to property and life of the swaggering bands of predators against whom medieval villages and towns had no defence.

Laws were framed to meet the menace of wandering thieves, and the return of soldiers discharged at the end of overseas campaigns, but there were also those who moved about the land because their livelihoods had been ruined by crop failure, or by war, eviction or oppression. Epidemics, and the enclosure of land by greedy and powerful landlords, put many more on the road, and these displaced people had to hope for charity or turn to crime in order to subsist. Parishes were at pains to move on travellers who would become a burden, and although there was limited tolerance of women regarded as respectable and their children, able-bodied men were greatly suspected, not least because also on the road were those whose temperaments, personalities and deeds had led to their banishment from their homes. Bullies, drunks, and thieves were hard to distinguish from the honest poor – perhaps until too late. For their own security, bodies of people would join together in their travels: 'Hark, hark, the dogs do bark, the beggars are coming to town . . .'

Laws – at first largely symbolic – were drafted against these people. A statute of 1426 prescribed three days in the stocks for a first vagrancy offence, doubled to six days the second time. Eighty years later the penalty dropped to one day for a first-timer,

and three for a second. Infirm and aged wanderers,
the law said, should not be put in the stocks at all.

A major source of support for the poor ended
just as a period of enclosure began. From 1536 the
monasteries were dissolved by Henry VIII, and their
assets of buildings and land stripped by speculators
and exploiters. The poor were denied even the
subsistence which the monks had provided. The
laws became more severe; beggars and vagrants
were to be whipped and returned home, then second
offenders were to have their ears cropped, and a third
offence would bring hanging as a felon.

Both to escape their poverty, and the menace
of rural justices, more and more rootless people
made their way to the capital. It has been estimated
that at a time when London had a population of
70–80,000 it received a further 12,000 desperately
poor immigrants from the land. Crude repression
could never hope to deal with such pressure. There
were proclamations against new building, to try to
prevent shanty-town overcrowding; and hospitals,
maisons dieu, abiding places and the first houses of
correction were created.

In 1572 magistrates were required to commit
'rogues, vagabonds and sturdy beggars to the
common jail, *or such other places as shall be appointed*',
with the comment that 'the common jails, in every
shire within the realm, are likely to be greatly
pestered with a more number of prisoners than
heretofore'. Two years later, the justices were
directed to provide 'houses or places, convenient
in some market or corporate town . . . and to be
called Houses of Correction'. Relief of the poor
and punishment of rogues had become entangled.
In 1597 whipping was added 'until his or her body

be bloody'; further pressure was applied to justices in 1609 – they had to build houses of correction or pay a fine, and they were to ensure that the work of inmates made the houses self-supporting.

Bridewell had been one of the first of the new institutions, and gave its name to the very idea, for which enormous enthusiasm grew among the troubled rulers and administrators. In a speech from the throne James I urged them all to 'Look to the Houses of Correction'.

But the confusion of purpose continued. If Bridewell was for the relief of the poor, why did it take Puritans, and Catholics, and Spanish prisoners of war? If it was a prison, why did it house orphans? The counties were obliged to build houses for paupers, but encouraged by example to use them as gaols.

Looking at London's houses of correction, it seems that the later they were built, the further they departed from ideas of redemption through work, from Bridewell to Wandsworth. Fourteen years after Wandsworth opened, in 1865, the formal distinction was removed. In law, as in reality, they were all to be prisons.

The regime also made great use of physical punishment. Prostitutes and vagrants were whipped on arrival, with twelve lashes for adults and six for juveniles, while disobedience and other offences were punished by further flogging.

Although today it must seem that any place in which people were forcibly detained, and subjected to whipping and forced labour, is a prison, the authorities of the time distinguished between the reforming discipline and orderliness of Bridewell and the chaotic, perilous squalor of the gaols of the time. Imprisonment was the last degree of punishment, for those whom even the Bridewell regime could not reform. Bridewell was considered a new type of institution, genuinely charitable in the health care it provided for the sick, and the schooling and apprenticeships provided for generations of blue-uniformed children; but for the vagrant and petty offender it came to be seen as no more than another prison. Captives from the Spanish Armada were held here, and Bridewell was among the prisons used to hold both Catholics and Protestants in times of religious persecution. Later, the vagrants were joined by those convicted locally of criminal offences. Bridewell and the other institutions modelled upon it (*see* Houses of Correction) began to lose their special character as their regimes grew ever closer to prison conditions, while prisons increasingly imposed hard labour on convicts. For a time there were disputes about the legality of locking up those whose only offence was to be poor and homeless, with Sir Francis Bacon claiming that the powers used to detain in Bridewell were an infringement of Magna Carta, but these objections faded.

Like the prisons and Bedlam, Bridewell became a novelty, a diversion for the curious and those whose appetites ran to watching the flogging of half-naked women. At first, whippings were carried out 'in a small room, hung with black, situated in the south-west corner of the courtroom . . . When the chairman considered that justice had been well and duly done to the back of the prisoner (male or female), he brought down his gavel smartly on the table . . .' Sir Thomas Middleton, who was president of Bridewell for eighteen years in the early seventeenth century, was often implored by prisoners to 'Knock, Sir Thomas, knock!', and this cry was shouted after him in the streets. Bridewell whippings became so popular that a balustraded gallery was built in the courtroom to hold all the onlookers.

The combination of punishment and philanthropy went on: a ducking-stool was installed in 1628, and stocks ten years later, yet orphans of City Freemen and other poor children were housed within the palace and their futures assured by placing them in good apprenticeships.

Most of the old palace was destroyed in the Great Fire, to be rebuilt between 1666 and 1667, and the new Bridewell continued much as before. It was often the first to introduce minor reforms: in 1675 a schoolmaster was hired to teach the apprentices and in 1700 a doctor was appointed (fully seventy-five years before any other prison made such an appointment). In 1788 Bridewell became the first prison to supply bedding, though only straw, and three years later the flogging of females was abolished. At a time when Howard and Neild had reported on the state of prisons, Bridewell established a weekly inspection, and a new wing was added in 1797.

Brought under state control in 1833, the prison was closed in 1855, and all its prisoners were transferred to Holloway.

The Site Now
The main entrance to Bridewell was on the east of the palace, on what is now New Bridge Street, between Ludgate Circus and Blackfriars Bridge. The building closest to the old gateway, No 14, carries a keystone of the head of Edward VI, who originally gave the palace to the poor.

THE SAVOY

This was a prison in central London designed by Sir Christopher Wren, a military gaol within an ancient palace.

The palace was built in the thirteenth century for Edmund, Earl of Lancaster on land between the Strand and the Thames, close to the present Savoy Hotel. The Savoy name was taken from a French monastery which had earlier owned, though never occupied the site. Edmund fortified his palace, and his successor, the 1st Duke of Lancaster, spent lavishly making the house into one of the most magnificent in the land.

The house passed to John of Gaunt by marriage, and was attacked by the rebels of 1381. Although they loathed Gaunt, the insurgents were nonetheless not looters. Intending to destroy Gaunt's wealth, they threw into a fire boxes which proved to contain not gold but gunpowder, and the house was blown up, spreading the fire until the entire building was gutted.

The river wall was repaired but the site was otherwise left derelict until in 1505 Henry VII ordered the house to be rebuilt as a hospital for the poor. The management of the hospital became corrupt, and in time sold and sub-let buildings as town houses for the nobility and gentry, and business premises for tradesmen. Above all, the area became a warren of rooms in which offenders hid from the law, creating the sanctuary of Alsatia which was to last until 1697.

The quarter also came to be linked with the army and navy, as the hospital was several times taken over for use by soldiers and sailors, and barracks added. Wren's prison was built to take deserters and military offenders who were to be deported. Little has emerged of the army's use of the prison, and the prison may also have been used for civil prisoners, as Defoe listed it in 1709 among the public gaols. He called it The Dutchy, presumably from the Duchy of Lancaster. In 1776 the barracks burned down, but a print of 1793 shows the prison, which lasted a little longer.

The Site Now
The area was cleared in 1816–20 to make way for the approach road to Waterloo Bridge.

CLERKENWELL HOUSE OF DETENTION

In 1609 an Act of Parliament which required each county to build a house of correction on the model of Bridewell specified that a house be built 'together with mills, turns, cards and suchlike necessary implements to set the rogues or other such idle persons on work', and set a deadline. Should a county fail to provide a house of correction by Michaelmas Day 1611 'then every justice within such county shall forfeit for his neglect £5'. The Middlesex magistrates may have had to reach into their pockets: the Clerkenwell Bridewell was not to open until 1615.

Like other Bridewells, this prison became no more than another common gaol, seedy and corrupt, 'a great brothel, kept under the protection of the law for the emolument of its ministers'. Minor villains came and went, joined in times of persecution by a few Catholic priests. The prison gained rare publicity when Jack Sheppard contrived to escape by taking a file to his fetters and window bars. This was all the more remarkable because he took with him his mistress, Edgeworth Bess. She was famed for her bulk, which must have slowed their departure.

The prison was rebuilt between 1774 and 1775, but just five years later the Gordon rioters set it alight and released all the inmates. The restored prison was small: there were six wards each for men and women, and six day- and six night-rooms for apprentices. Clerkenwell may have specialized for some time in holding unruly youths – Pepys mentioned a riotous attack by apprentices in 1688.

The House of Detention, as it came to be known, took in those awaiting trial, army deserters, and many prisoners held awaiting sureties (money posted as a warranty of future good behaviour). A prisoner might wait months or even years before a surety was found; Clerkenwell also held cabmen who had offended against the Hackney Carriage Act, a powerful local by-law protecting passengers from overcharging and poor service.

Rebuilding and expansion, with major work in 1818 and 1845–6, produced a recognizable Victorian prison with blocks radiating from an administrative central block. About 240 prisoners could be held at any one time, but in the course of a year more than 7,000 – a couple of hundred of whom would be less than twelve years old – might pass through. Among them were unfortunates who would not today be regarded as offenders: in its last ten years Clerkenwell received 3,000 prisoners who had failed in attempts at suicide. In the first instance they were remanded to receive the advice of the prison chaplain, but many, usually those who had repeated their attempts, went on to serve prison sentences.

On 13 December 1867 a barrel of gunpowder placed against the outer wall of Clerkenwell exploded. The wall was breached, and the row of houses facing the prison largely demolished, killing six people and injuring fifty more. The bomb was intended to aid the escape of two prisoners – Colonel Ricard Burke and Joseph Casey – who were Fenians, members of the movement to eject the English from Ireland, and who had taken part in a campaign of violence in Ireland and on the mainland. The plan failed. Michael Barrett, who had planted the bomb, was captured, tried, and hanged outside Newgate on 26 May 1868, the last person to be executed publicly in England.

In 1877 Clerkenwell House of Detention was one of

the prisons closed when local prisons were placed under central control by the Prison Commissioners.

The Site Now
The site of Clerkenwell House of Detention is now occupied by Hugh Myddleton School in Woodbridge Street, behind the Green. The foundations and basement level of the prison were used in building the school and can still be seen today. In St James' Church nearby is a tablet commemorating the victims of the 1867 bomb.

COLDBATH FIELDS

> As he went through Coldbath Fields he saw
> A solitary cell:
> And the Devil was pleased, for it gave him a hint
> For improving his prisons in hell.
>
> *The Devil's Thoughts*, Southey and Coleridge

The prison took its name from one of the many wells along the Fleet. The original intention had been to provide a Bridewell or house of correction, in which vagrants could be held and put to work. The first crude square house was built in 1794, and was criticized as overpriced at more than £65,000 for 232 cells. The gateway was impressive, but the design of the building was poor; extensions and modifications were needed. Even the changes failed to find favour: a radial block was added, according to a new fashion in prison architecture, but it was 'designed ere the new lights on prison structure, derived from the United States, had penetrated into this kingdom. Consequently our new buildings were very defective, and much expense was subsequently incurred to amend and enlarge them.'

This was a prison for the county of Middlesex, but

the City authorities made a contribution to costs so that they too might have use of it. Like Bridewell itself, the original role and purpose were soon obscured, and Coldbath Fields became a gaol for petty offenders, of both sexes at first, but eventually only for men. The other Middlesex house of correction at Tothill Fields took female and juvenile male prisoners, and there seems to have been useful co-operation between the two institutions; the most influential governors at each prison were good friends who shared an enthusiasm for reform.

By the 1850s Coldbath Fields could find room in its complex buildings for 1,450 prisoners, and was operated by a staff of 122 officers. (A modern prison of comparable size employs three times as many uniformed staff, and a sizeable civilian staff in administration and instruction.) The regime was the silent associated system in which prisoners worked together, and as at Tothill Fields there was great regret that there could not be single cells for each prisoner to complete the isolation. At Coldbath Fields the governor tried posting officers in the dormitories each night to prevent conversation.

Labour at Coldbath Fields – to a greater degree than in other prisons – was intended only as punishment with no concern to teach skills, any useful effects being merely a by-product. There were six treadwheel yards with a total of twenty wheels. When the first wheels were installed there was a gross miscalculation of the exertion that could be demanded of a prisoner. Each man was required to achieve 12,000 feet of ascent each day (that is, the sum of all his paces on his wheel). This put the health of the inmates in jeopardy, and even the Royal Artillery refused to send its offenders here because they returned unfit for service. Instead of reconsidering the level of work the prison promoted 'a prolonged indulgence in a daily allowance of beer, increased diet, and . . . other prescribed stimulants'. When common sense prevailed, and the experience of other prisons was taken into account, the daily target was reduced to 1,200 feet a day.

Despite Coldbath Fields having been built at a time of reform, it gave the impression of wobbly thinking and practice. The buildings and labour regime were poorly conceived, and the early management was both brutal and almost comically corrupt. One governor formed the habit of striding around with a knotted rope ready to lay into prisoners who displeased him; one of his successors was astounded to find evidence everywhere of staff corruption. There were stores of 'wine and spirits, tea and coffee, tobacco and pipes . . . and even pickles, preserves and fish sauce'.

Henry Mayhew, one of the most thorough of observers, gives glimpses of prison life in the 1850s. Guns were fired to signal the start of the day's work; a prisoner could receive a letter and a visit only once every three months; prisoners' clothes were fumigated on their arrival; prisoners spent hours in 'shot-drill', the perfectly pointless lifting and carrying of cannon balls up and down and round and round a yard; the treadmill was linked to no useful device, but merely a fan, in an exercise known as 'grinding the wind'; placards were everywhere displayed with vacuous mottoes such as 'BEHOLD HOW GOOD AND PLEASANT IT IS FOR BRETHREN TO DWELL TOGETHER IN UNITY'. It was also Mayhew who pointed out that half the prisoners were there not because they had committed serious crimes, but because they could not pay even very small fines.

A respectable visitor, rather than a prisoner, gave the prison the nickname which stuck. At first called the Bastille for its formidable appearance, this was soon shortened to 'the Steel'; although the title overstates the importance of the gaol. It held few prisoners of any importance, except for the Cato Street conspirators, who were there for a few days in 1820 on their way to the Tower. The many thousands of others who passed through were merely petty offenders. However, for all its rigours, it cannot be said that the regime was a deterrent: at any one time at least a third of the prisoners were serving a second or subsequent sentence.

Coldbath Fields was closed in 1877 when local prisons were taken under state control.

The Site Now
The Mount Pleasant postal sorting office, on the north-east corner of the junction of Farringdon Street and Rosebery Avenue, covers the site of Coldbath Fields Prison.

WESTMINSTER

INTRODUCTION

Westminster, a centre of government since Edward the Confessor built his palace there in the eleventh century, has also been the home of the highest courts in the land for most of London's history since the Conquest. Kings administered justice personally or through the courts and tribunals attached to the royal household. The jurisdictions of these bodies were wide, and often competed with each other, and they derived their power and titles from the official who presided – the King's Bench, the Marshalsea, Chancery – or from the types of case they would hear, such as Common Pleas or Exchequer.

These courts were not separate buildings. From the thirteenth century until 1882 all were housed in Westminster Hall, which survives within the present Houses of Parliament. Here the minor disputes of countless litigants were brought, as well as the major state trials. Charles I was tried and condemned here, under the same hammer-beam roof as Anne Boleyn and Guy Fawkes had been.

Although the fate of prisoners was decided in Westminster Hall, they were not usually confined at Westminster, with the occasional exception of those sent to the Gatehouse: Westminster was used in times of peace and security, with no fortress or defences.

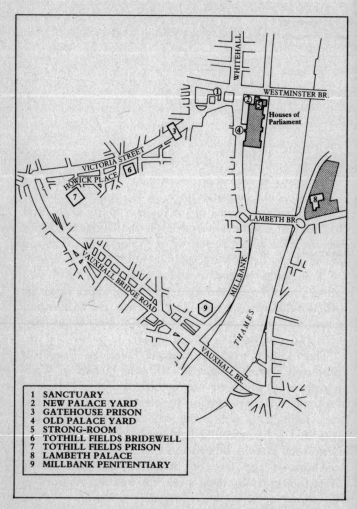

1 SANCTUARY
2 NEW PALACE YARD
3 GATEHOUSE PRISON
4 OLD PALACE YARD
5 STRONG-ROOM
6 TOTHILL FIELDS BRIDEWELL
7 TOTHILL FIELDS PRISON
8 LAMBETH PALACE
9 MILLBANK PENITENTIARY

Westminster

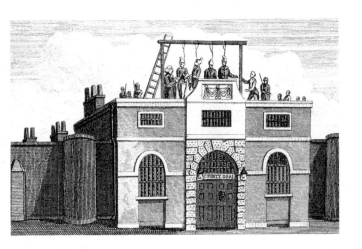

Placing the scaffold on the roof of Horsemonger Lane Gaol provided better security, and a better view for the crowd.

Chained together, an early group of convicts is led from Newgate to Blackfriars for transportation to Virginia.

ABOVE: *Prison hulks were little modified for their new role, and poorly maintained.*

BELOW: *The treadmill at Pentonville. The seated prisoners were taking a break during which they were encouraged to read improving books, while the tallies of the men on the mill hang on pegs beside each cubicle.*

During the silent
hour at Brixton
women were set to
chores. It is not hard
to imagine the
whispers and mutters
along the galleries.

ABOVE LEFT: *This view shows Wandsworth as first built. Further wings were added to each of the blocks, and the watchtowers around the walls – which also provided housing for officers – have long gone.*

ABOVE: *New prisoners arriving at Wormwood Scrubs in a horse-drawn Black Maria.*

LEFT: *Exterior of the City House of Correction at Holloway.*

ABOVE LEFT: *Exposed in the stocks together, these may have been warring spouses, an unruly prostitute and client, or adulterers.*

ABOVE: *This illustration from Foxe's* Book of Martyrs *is typical of the many images of martyrdom used to keep both Protestant and Catholic hatred and suspicion alive.*

LEFT: *In Old Palace Yard the Gunpowder Plotters were put to death. Drawn first on hurdles, they were hanged until close to death and then quartered – butchered alive.*

The last stage of the road to Tyburn. Awaiting Hogarth's *Idle Apprentice* are the hangman, lounging with his pipe on top of the Triple Tree, and the crowds on the grandstand. With the wretch in the cart are his own coffin, and a loud preacher, while in the foreground a woman is already selling a sheet claiming to hold the Apprentice's dying speech.

Whenever internal or invading forces threatened, the monarch retreated behind the walls of the Tower or moved the household to Windsor or beyond.

There was only a small local population until well into the eighteenth century, because beyond the area immediately around the palace and abbey was marshy land unsuitable for substantial building, and within that area the landowners, the Dean and Chapter of the Abbey, refused to sell or grant long leases, so that only the cheapest, most poorly maintained, housing was to be found.

Until the monstrous Millbank Penitentiary was built, the prisons of Westminster served only the limited parochial needs of this impoverished district. The expansion of the Tothill Fields prison gives a measure of the westward expansion of London.

THE GATEHOUSE

Stone walls do not a prison make,
Nor iron bars a cage;
Minds innocent and quiet take
That for an hermitage:
If I have freedom in my love
And in my soul am free,
Angels alone, that soar above,
Enjoy such liberty.

The final verse of *To Althea from Prison*, written by Richard Lovelace when a prisoner in the Gatehouse (1642)

In 1370 Walter Warfield, Cellarer to Westminster Abbey, built a gatehouse of two wings at right angles to each other, each with a gate, each with a gaol. The section which ran to the north was the Bishop of London's prison for 'clerks convict', subject to church law; the other was for lay offenders. The whole was run by the Abbey Janitor, for an official salary of a daily ration of bread and ale, and a new robe annually.

This was a small prison, but being close to Westminster Hall it made a convenient lodging-place for state prisoners. It was here that Raleigh spent his last night, transferred from the Tower to be executed in Old Palace Yard (1618). Pepys spent three weeks here in 1690 'on suspicion of being affected to King James', but was released when he fell ill.

A tradition at Westminster School nearby provided an odd source of income for those held in the Gatehouse. Any boy found playing with money during school hours was sent under escort to place the coins in the prisoners' alms box by the door of the gaol.

Described as affording good lodging rooms and diet by John Taylor in 1623, this was another prison which was allowed to decay, and in 1761 Dr Johnson was moved to write that it was 'so offensive that, without any particular reason, it ought to be pulled down, for it disgraces the present magnificence of the capital, and is a continual nuisance to neighbours and passengers'. The Dean and Chapter of Westminster Abbey ordered the prison's demolition in 1776, but having cleared a wider passage for traffic, the single remaining wall was abandoned, and stood for another seventy years. Tothill Fields Bridewell was expanded to accommodate the displaced prisoners.

The Site Now

The Gatehouse was very close to Westminster Abbey. In Broad Sanctuary, in front of the Abbey's bookstall, is a memorial to old boys of Westminster School killed in the Crimea – the prison stood there, branching north towards the Central Hall.

TOTHILL FIELDS

If place could exist of which it could be said that it was in *no* neighbourhood, that place would be Tothill Fields.

Jeremy Bentham (1798)

Like much of Westminster the area known as Tothill Fields (roughly the land between today's Victoria Street and the river) was marshy, unattractive and with few sound spots on which substantial houses might be built. Culpeper the herbalist thought it an excellent place to grow parsley, but the meadows had other more sinister use: trials by battle and duels were held here. It was chosen as a place to quarantine plague victims, and to bury them when the disease had run its course. Twelve hundred Scottish prisoners taken by parliamentary forces at the Battle of Worcester were brought here in 1651, to die of neglect and starvation. Those buried in the Fields may just have been luckier than their fellows who were sold from here into slavery in Barbados.

The Bridewell

In 1618 the Westminster Justices ordered the building of Tothill Fields Bridewell. As the name implies, this was a house of correction for vagrants and petty offenders who were to be put to work, and whipped if they slacked. A local prison, it was supported by the rates, but also by the profits made on its products. The first keeper was a hempdresser by trade, contracted to provide raw material and supervisors for the captive workforce. In 1725 *The Town Spy*, Ned Ward's guide to London life, carried a wry description: 'In the fields of this parish stands a famous factory for hemp, which is wrought with greater interest than ordinary, because the manufacturers enjoy the fruits of their own labour, a number of English gentlemen having here a restraint put upon their liberties.' Not only gentlemen: the women shown beating hemp in Hogarth's *The Rake's Progress* were observed by him when he visited this Bridewell in 1747 looking for authentic details of prison life.

In the early years of the eighteenth century, like others, the Bridewell had come to be used as a common gaol as well as a punitive workhouse, and when the Gatehouse in Westminster was closed in 1777 the building was extended to take the extra prisoners. The reformer John Howard came to the prison at this time, and reported that he found it 'remarkably well managed', and held up the governor, George Smith, as an example to others. By the standards of the age the management certainly seems to have been enlightened and conscientious, with little corruption, and Howard's approval was echoed by Neild after his visit in 1802 – the only fault he recorded was badly smoking chimneys.

The feature of the prison which drew comment from

This bird's-eye view of Tothill Fields shows the vast formality of the prison, with more space apparently given to decorative gardens than to exercise yards.

visitors was the street door, the main entrance. Quite unlike the impressive gates of other prisons, this was a simple doorway just five feet ten inches high, and three feet wide, more like the entrance to a cottage than to an important public building. Over the lintel was a tablet inscribed:

> Here are several Sorts of Work
> For the Poor of this Parish of St
> Margaret, Westminster,
> As also the County according to
> LAW, and or such as will Beg and
> Live Idle in this City and Liberty
> Of Westminster,
> ANNO 1655

The Prison

The Bridewell, noted for the modest face it presented to the world, was replaced in 1834 by a prison whose appearance shouted its purpose. On a new eight-acre site further to the south-west, surrounded by a 'huge dead wall', Tothill Fields Prison had an entrance 'formed of massive granite blocks, and immense iron gates, ornamented above with portcullis work'.

The new prison was laid out as three half-wheel blocks, each following the panopticon principle of supervision from a central point and joined like the three lobes of an ace of clubs. The intent was that each block should have a separate function: the first a gaol for untried male prisoners, and debtors; the second a house of correction for male convicts; the third a women's gaol.

This was a large prison. There were 549 small cells (each half the volume of a Pentonville cell), and although a maximum intake of 900 prisoners was foreseen, this figure was often surpassed.

The design was not only unfashionable, at a time when

the radial plan was finding favour, but was poorly conceived and constructed. 'There is no concealing the fact', wrote one visitor, 'that this building is a huge and costly blunder.' Of the cells, another wrote: 'the construction . . . is about as defective, in a sanitary point of view, as can well be imagined, the prison being unprovided with any apparatus, not only for ensuring perfect ventilation . . . but even for warming and lighting the cells in the long winter nights.' The mortality rate among prisoners here was in fact much lower than in other London prisons, and it seems that the continuing local tradition made up for some of the deficiencies in the buildings.

The shape of the prison may have been outmoded, but the regime was very much of its time. The easy ways of the older prison were replaced by the silent associated system (*see* Separation and Silence). Prisoners spent their days working together, but were prevented from speaking or communicating with each other. There was dismay that overcrowding resulted in prisoners sharing a cell talking at night – how could they enjoy the undoubted benefits of silent solitary contemplation, if each day's spiritual progress could be lost by morning?

They felt that large multi-purpose prisons were inefficient, poor savers of souls, since they placed juveniles, debtors, and the unconvicted in great peril of contamination when lodged with experienced criminals. Having come to these conclusions, the Middlesex authorities decided to make better use of their three prisons. In 1845 the untried and the debtors left Tothill Fields, and five years later a clear arrangement was reached by which Clerkenwell would hold those awaiting trial, Coldbath Fields would take convicted adult males, and Tothill Fields would take all females and convicted males under the age of seventeen.

The female prison was normally full to its capacity of 600, sometimes taking more, with 40 per cent of prisoners sharing cramped dormitories. The previous good management had decayed by this stage: the rates of sickness and punishment here were much higher than in other female prisons. Prisoners were put to work, and although there was still oakum-picking for many of them, constructive labour was encouraged. Laundry was taken in from other prisons, bonnets were made for the patients in Hanwell lunatic asylum, and there was also knitting: 'The knitting-room . . . is remarkable only for its slanting, pew-like arrangement – an elaborate piece of absurdity, designed by some wiseacre . . . to prevent the female prisoners talking, but which, owing to the high wooden partition at the back of each row acting as a sounding-board, has served as the best possible contrivance for allowing them to communicate in secret.'

Henry Mayhew, author of that quotation, was even more scathing about the boys' section of Tothill Fields:

If it were not for the pathos of the place, we really believe that this boys' prison would rank as the greatest laughing-stock of the age; for here one finds all the pompous paraphernalia of Visiting Justices, and Governors and Warders, with bunches of keys dangling from thick chains, and strings of cutlasses hanging over the mantelpiece of the entrance-office – and all to take care of the little desperate malefactors, not one of whom has cut his 'wisdom teeth'; whilst many are so young that they seem better fitted to be conveyed to the place in a perambulator, than in the lumbering and formidable prison van.

Tothill Fields survived a little longer than many of the prisons nationalized in 1877, but it was closed and demolished in 1884.

The Site Now

The sites of both establishments are easily found: where the Bridewell once stood is now the Army and Navy department store, and the Catholic Westminster Cathedral not only covers the site of the prison, but stands on foundations laid for the prison.

The remarkable small doorway from the Bridewell was preserved, and was at one time kept in the basement of Middlesex Guildhall in Parliament Square. The Guildhall is at the time of writing under reconstruction.

HOUSE OF COMMONS

Within the Palace of Westminster is the smallest of London's gaols, a single room which ranks as a state prison alongside the Tower.

Either House of Parliament may order a person guilty of contempt of the House to be detained, either in one of Her Majesty's prisons or in the custody of one of two parliamentary officers – Black Rod or the Sergeant at Arms. If the offender is not to go to prison, detention is in a room in the lower part of the Clock Tower, once known as the 'strong-room'.

It is rarely used, and no Member of Parliament has been committed to the room for more than a century, but anyone creating a disturbance (such as demonstrators in one of the galleries) may be confined there, in theory for the remainder of that Parliament's session for the Commons, or without limit for the Lords. Since the session may still have some weeks to run, this is obviously not a very practical sentence, and most commonly offenders are held briefly to cool down (an apology to the House is sometimes required), or taken away by the police on a more mundane charge.

The Site Now
The room lies within a part of the Palace included in a tour which takes parties to see Big Ben. Arrangements to join such a party are made through Members of Parliament.

SANCTUARY

I order and establish for ever, that what person, of what condition or estate soever he be, from whence soever he come, or for what offence or cause it be, either for his refuge into this holy place, he be assured of his life, liberty and limbs. And over this I forbid, under the pain of everlasting damnation, that no minister of mine, or of my successors, intermeddle them with and the goods, lands or possessions of the said persons taking the said sanctuary . . .

In these strong terms Edward the Confessor reaffirmed the powerful sanctuary of Westminster Abbey and its precincts, created by previous Saxon kings. This local privilege persisted after the Reformation, and was abolished in 1623, and Broad Sanctuary and Little Sanctuary survive as street names today.

Here as nowhere else in London was a very fortress of sanctuary. Where the Guildhall now stands in Parliament Square was a massive blockhouse, seventy-five feet square, sixty feet high: St Peter's Sanctuary, or the Westminster City of Refuge.

This was a tower for offenders and debtors, as strong as a prison, but to preserve them from arrest. A church might be blockaded to starve out a fugitive, unarmed clergy might in a less robust building fail to hold off angry pursuers, but here was defence against anything less than full military assault, and powerful warning of the dangers of sacrilege.

Sanctuary could be found in all churches, and in other

buildings and areas given a charter or grant by the monarch. Where no specific charter existed, the church, or general sanctuary, was a refuge only to felons who faced execution if arrested. On arrival the fugitive had to declare that he had committed felony (only sacrilege was excluded). He could then, within forty days, go clothed in sackcloth to a coroner, confess his guilt, and take an oath to leave the kingdom forever: only by licence of the king would he be permitted to return. He then had a further forty days in which to make arrangements for his departure, the coroner would nominate the port from which he must embark, and with a cross in his hand, he could go into exile. If he did not travel directly to the named port, or returned without a licence, he would be condemned to hang, unless he was a clerk (*see* Benefit of Clergy).

When taking sanctuary, the fugitive had to wear a badge proclaiming his status, and submit to various restrictions, but these were obviously preferable to capture. Houses within a sanctuary precinct always commanded high rents. Not that sanctuary was always effective: it did not apply to anyone who had already been condemned and delivered to the sheriff for execution, yet escaped, and there were occasional examples down the years of offenders dragged from sanctuary. In 1378 Robert Hawley escaped from the Tower and, chased to the Abbey by the Tower constable, was killed in the choir during High Mass. The constable and his followers were excommunicated for this deed, and the church was closed for four months as an expression of the Archbishop's wrath.

The charters granted to sanctuaries seem often to have done no more than recognize a status quo; if it was impossible to penetrate an area to arrest offenders, the practical view must have been that the neighbourhood might as well be an official sanctuary. The most famous, and the last to be suppressed, were Alsatia and the Southwark Mint. Alsatia (nicknamed after Alsace's long history as disputed territory) was the area between Fleet Street and the Thames, and was also known as Whitefriars after the monastery which had originally offered sanctuary. The abolition of the Southwark sanctuary was spectacular: debts of less than £50 were to be written off, and other amnesties for offenders were offered, with the result that in July 1723 a caravan of thousands set off on foot, horse and cart to the Guildford Quarter Sessions where they were cleared of their obligations.

Even after a sanctuary lost official status, it would usually remain the haunt of thieves and rogues, becoming the 'rookeries' of Dickens' time, warrens of houses with interconnecting secret doors and passages through which criminals could flee. Not until entire neighbourhoods were demolished and developed at the end of the last century did these extraordinary anthills of crime disappear.

MILLBANK PENITENTIARY

The immense yellow-brown mass of brick-work is surrounded by a low wall of the same material, above which is seen a multitude of small squarish windows, and a series of diminutive roofs of slate, like low retreating foreheads. There is a systematic irregularity about the in-and-out aspect of the building, which gives it the appearance of a gigantic puzzle; and altogether the Millbank prison may be said to be one of the most successful realizations, on a large scale, of the ugly in architecture, being an ungainly combination of the madhouse with the fortress style of building, for it has a series of martello-like towers, one at each end of its many angles, and was originally surrounded by a moat, whilst its long lines of embrasure-like windows are barred, after the fashion of Bedlam and St Luke's.

For most of the nineteenth century Millbank Penitentiary

loomed on the bank of the Thames near Pimlico. It was Britain's first National Penitentiary, and a monstrous – and monstrously expensive – failure.

In 1812 the Government bought the land on which Jeremy Bentham had proposed to build his Panopticon, and embarked on the construction of a prison to a design chosen by competition. It is often said that this was a modification of Bentham's design. It was not. The only elementary similarity was that from central vantage points rings of cell blocks could be observed; otherwise, where Bentham's design had been bold in overall plan and only fussy in detail, Millbank was over-elaborate in both.

As first built, the penitentiary had an outer octagonal wall surrounded by a moat, which may be effective in keeping people out, but not much use for keeping people in. Within the octagonal wall were pentagonal blocks, laid out hexagonally. This geometrical complexity enclosed miles of corridor with 'angles every twenty yards, winding staircases, dark passages, innumerable doors and gates . . .'; one prison officer who had worked there for many years still found it impossible to find his way around and 'carried with him always a piece of chalk, with which he "blazed" his path as does the American backwoodsman the forest trees'.

Millbank was opened in June 1816. On 25 June a party of nobles and notables were shown around the prison, and at three o'clock the next morning the first forty prisoners – all women – arrived, having been '. . . carried in caravans, chained together, from Newgate to Blackfriars-bridge, there put on board a barge prepared to receive them, and conveyed under a strong guard of police-officers to Millbank'.

The prison design was expanded beyond the original plans, with single cells for 1,000 prisoners. As a penitentiary Millbank seems never to have held more than 700 prisoners, as it was the intention that only those prisoners most likely to benefit from the regime should go there. Only in later years, when it was used as a conventional prison, did it hold 1,500 or more.

This penitentiary was to be different from other London prisons not only in the novelty of its buildings, but in the intent and style of its regime. Following the ethos expressed in the Penitentiary Act forty years before, heavy emphasis was placed on the values of work, religion, and separate confinement. The work was arduous, but quite well-paid: convicts were even allowed to work overtime, and might accumulate as much as £17 – three months' pay for many workers – before release. The emphasis on religious observance was less useful. 'As the most successful simulator of holiness became the most favoured prisoner, sanctified looks were, as a matter of course, the order of the day, and the most desperate convicts in the prison found it advantageous to complete their criminal character by the addition of hypocrisy,' wrote Mayhew.

Emphasis on a reforming regime gave unusual power to the prison chaplain. The Reverend Whitworth Russell, who was to go on to have great influence as an inspector of prisons, worked at Millbank in the 1830s, and complained bitterly that the governor was too generous and slack. He had his own way in 1837 when, as an inspector, he was able to appoint the Reverend Daniel Nihil as chaplain-governor. The unpleasant Nihil was unyielding even by the standards of prison clergy. Challenged with evidence that strict separation was destroying prisoners' sanity, he protested that the separation was not strict enough: 'What I object to is a nominal separation accompanied with secret fraudulent communication. Health is certainly a consideration, but are morals less?' It was also in Nihil's time that a scandal broke about three small girls, two aged ten and a third just seven-and-a-half, who had been kept in solitary confinement for twelve months and faced two more years of the same; the public was much moved by an account of the smallest child begging for a doll at bedtime, which was refused.

The supervision of this national prison lay with a committee whose members were all socially prominent, and who sincerely wanted to reform criminals. 'Millbank was a huge plaything; a toy for a parcel of philanthropic gentlemen to keep them busy during their spare hours. It was easy to see . . . that they loved to run in and out of the place and show it off to their friends.' The frequent changes of governor in the penitentiary's first years gave the committee a greater influence, but time and again all the managers failed to rise to serious challenges.

The design of the building, and its poor quality of construction, might have been overcome by efficient and methodical practices, but the minds of the administrators seem always to have been on abstract theory, above the most elementary concern for the welfare of prisoners. Epidemics of scurvy and cholera swept through Millbank in 1822 and 1823, and it required an Act of Parliament to clear the prison, pardoning the women and sending the men to the hulks. None of the promised reduction in recidivism (further offending by prisoners) was realized; the physical and mental health of inmates was dreadfully neglected. Millbank was a failure, and far from being a model which later prisons might follow was seen as an embarrassing encumbrance. When the second penitentiary was built at Pentonville between 1840 and 1842, it was to a totally different design.

The opening of Pentonville allowed Millbank to be relegated to the role of a convict depot, a clearing house in which prisoners could be held for much shorter periods for assessment before transfer to other establishments. The separate system continued, and labour was still to be useful, but the regime was diluted, according to the purists, by the introduction of associated silent work on some wings. As if to concede how thoroughly he and his ideas had been discredited, the Reverend Whitworth Russell killed himself within Millbank in 1847.

Even in its new role the prison was a burden. Still damp, depressing and costly, it saw only one significant change in its depot years. In 1868, when Roman Catholic priests were permitted to become prison chaplains for the first time, and anti-Popery opposition from Anglican chaplains was powerful, it was thought tactically prudent to concentrate Catholic convicts in the few prisons with Catholic chaplains – Millbank was one of these.

Millbank became a military prison in 1870, and closed in 1890, to remain abandoned until its demolition in 1903.

The Site Now
The site of Millbank is easily found: the Tate Gallery occupies much of the grounds, and the remainder lies beneath the Royal Army Medical College next door. In the mess courtyard of the college stand steel bollards once used to moor the barges which brought convicts to the prison, and the ships which transported them to the colonies.

Across Millbank, close to the river, is a plaque commemorating the many thousands who were taken from here to Australia.

SOUTHWARK

INTRODUCTION

If there is a modern equivalent of early Southwark it might well be Tijuana, the seedy town just south of the Mexican–American border. Each settlement has made its living by becoming the pleasure-ground for a more closely regulated community to the north, and allowed fugitives from its neighbour to take shelter. The Thames may not be the Rio Grande, but medieval Southwark certainly had a Wild West atmosphere. In the taverns, brothels and gaming-houses of Bankside sudden violence was common, and its causes were the stuff of cowboy films: having driven cattle to town, the unwary would take their pay and go in search of a good time, only to meet a greedy lady of pleasure, a card-sharp or a bully. Stage-coaches would arrive with their drivers and passengers robbed or wounded, after an ambush by masked men lurking by the roadside.

This was the flavour of Southwark life for centuries. It was an area which grew as a parasite of the City across the water. The Romans built a bridge across the Thames very soon after their arrival in 43 A.D., almost exactly on the site of succeeding London Bridges, and at its southern bridgehead a settlement grew which offered entertainment and spectacle. The Romans themselves may have set this

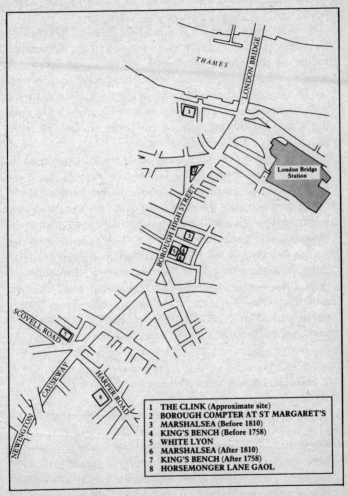

1   **THE CLINK (Approximate site)**
2   **BOROUGH COMPTER AT ST MARGARET'S**
3   **MARSHALSEA (Before 1810)**
4   **KING'S BENCH (Before 1758)**
5   **WHITE LYON**
6   **MARSHALSEA (After 1810)**
7   **KING'S BENCH (After 1758)**
8   **HORSEMONGER LANE GAOL**

pattern: a gladiator's trident has been found in Southwark which may be a relic of an arena or circus on the South Bank.

Farmers took livestock and produce through to London; travellers from the southern counties and the Continent lodged in the inns of Southwark (there was a curfew for traffic on the bridge, and late arrivals and early starters were obliged to spend the night south of the river). For all these, and for Londoners seeking amusements forbidden within the City, Southwark offered not only private pleasure but theatres, including Shakespeare's Globe, bear- and bull-baiting, and a substantial market. For criminals it was long a sanctuary from the officers of the City, even after the City gained jurisdiction over the area in 1556.

Southwark's half-dozen prisons were for the most part a tumbledown assortment of adapted and requisitioned buildings and parts of buildings, shabbier counterparts of the gaols north of the river. The Surrey magistrates who came to administer the prisons were no less enlightened than their City and Middlesex fellows, and the two establishments – Brixton and Wandsworth – which they commissioned to replace the ancient Southwark gaols, have survived to this day.

THE CLINK

clink n.(sl.) Prison (esp **in clink**) *Concise Oxford Dictionary*

There have been larger London prisons, and several that have lasted longer, but no other whose name came to stand for all prisons. Looking for a name for a prison warder in *Peveril Of The Peak*, Sir Walter Scott had only to hit on Jem Clink to establish the character in the minds of his readers.

The word has lived on because it evokes thoughts of chains and locks, and this is the most likely origin of the name itself. Whether from the Dutch *klinken*, meaning to lock or fasten, or Middle English *clench* or *clinc* (fastened, as with a rivet – a clinching-iron was used to fasten chains, manacles and fetters), the name attached to one of the earlier Southwark prisons, and in time to other gaols.

The Clink began as a section of the palace of the Bishop of Winchester on the south bank of the Thames in Southwark. On land granted by Henry I in 1127, Bishop William Gifford built a magnificent home with 'a great park and gardens: on the north side flowed the Thames beneath a noble river terrace'. In the style of the time, it would have combined strength and comfort, and had cells in which the Bishop could lodge offenders against ecclesiastical codes such as priests, monks and lay clerks, who were exempted by Benefit of Clergy from punishment by lay courts.

As Lord of the Manor the Bishop had great power, from the creation of local laws to the appointment of officials and administration of justice, and his prison was just a part of the machinery of his power.

The Southwark land was the Liberty of the See of Winchester, one of the great playgrounds of London, famous for its brothels and shady inns, which the Bishop licensed and supervised, and from which he derived a vast income. From the regulations he drew up in 1161 we know that his prison was already in use, taking those who were disorderly in and around the brothels, and disciplining the prostitutes. One feature of the Liberty, and other church holdings such as St Martin le Grand in the City, was the Sanctuary provided against civil law, and this must have attracted many unsavoury folk who had already offended elsewhere. At the end of the twelfth century this advice was offered by a Winchester monk to a visitor:

Do not associate with the crowds of pimps; do not mingle with throngs in the eating houses; avoid the dicing and the gambling and the theatre and the taverns . . . the number of parasites is infinite. Actors, jesters, smooth-skinned lads, Moors, flatterers, pretty-boys, effeminates, paederasts, singing and dancing girls, belly dancers, quacks, sorceresses, extortioners, magicians, night-wanderers, mimes, beggars and buffoons – all this tribe fill the houses.

Of all these, the Bishop had the greatest interest in curbing pimps – they might take revenues due to himself.

All traces of the first building were covered when a great Gothic palace replaced it in the fourteenth century. This was built around a square; the northern block, closest to the river and fronting on to the present Clink Street held the Great Hall, some outbuildings, and a new prison built in the cellar, ready for an expanded clientele. Creditors could now have debtors committed to prison (*see* Imprisonment for Debt), and the Clink was to become famous as a debtors' prison.

In 1381 the Kentish rebels of the Peasants' Revolt occupied Southwark, and attacked the Bishop's palace, releasing all the Clink's inmates; seventy years later the followers of Jack Cade, another populist insurgent, did just the same.

After centuries of dubious profiteering, the Bishops of Winchester fell upon hard times in the early sixteenth century. They had spent lavishly, and when fear of the spread of syphilis led Henry VII to close the brothels in 1504, there was a financial crisis. Although business resumed the next year, the power of the Bishop had dwindled: the palace was dilapidated, and the prison used more and more as a common gaol. All was not lost, however. The next Bishop of Winchester, also Archbishop of Canterbury, was the resourceful Stephen Gardiner. Much favoured by Henry VIII, he had a reputation for spending too much time with his own whores, but seems to have cemented his friendship with the King by providing a supply of these 'Winchester geese' for the royal pleasure. It worked: as the monasteries were being dissolved, and church properties seized, Gardiner not only held on to the Liberty but was able to restore the palace – at least the floors above the prison – and even to make it more luxurious.

When Edward VI came to the throne in 1547, Gardiner lost his royal protection, was himself imprisoned in the Fleet as a potential enemy of the King, and seemed likely to lose his palace. In the hope that he could bring the influential Archbishop to support him, the King delayed seizure. Time ran out – for the King, not the wily Gardiner: Edward died in 1533, and Gardiner, who had lived in style even behind bars, returned to his palace.

Queen Mary not only released and restored the Archbishop, but made him her Lord Chancellor, and placed him in charge of her campaign against the Protestants. He relished the work, in which his prison would play a part.

At some point the Archbishop relocated the prison, perhaps during the refurbishing of the palace. Prisoners were now held in three low, linked buildings close to the palace, but we cannot know whether these were newly-built or were taverns or other buildings taken over for the purpose, as was common at the time. Protestants were confined, starved and abused in this new gaol, and from here led out to execution. With the accession of Elizabeth to the throne in 1588 similar treatment was given to obstinate Catholics – the recusants – and amid the doctrinal chaos, to extreme Protestants as well.

The Clink was the principal prison for religious offences, but also continued as the local gaol for the lawless of Southwark and for debtors. It is difficult to imagine just how odd an assortment it must have held – prostitutes, priests, Puritans and the poor all under the same roof. Prisoners considered a danger to national security might be held separately, or merely shackled to the wall or floor; equally, the corruption of the gaolers could allow important prisoners to enjoy privileges and comfort. There is direct and bizarre evidence of this in a report of a raid on the Clink in 1626.

The Privy Council had ordered a search for priests, and at the Clink – the door to which was unmanned and open – the conscientious raiders found four priests, who had created within the prison a large library, set up two altars on which to celebrate Mass, and had in their possession enormous quantities of money, including more than one hundred pounds lying around in loose change! One priest had three servants, and from his room in the keeper's house had a private passageway to three more rooms. He had brought with him into the prison 'a Gentlewoman who has her own chamber next adjoining, and pays two shillings and sixpence a week and maintains a maidservant'. The irony here was that by renting a room in the prison, the lady had made herself safe from arrest as a recusant.

In the room of another priest were found all the keeper's financial records and accounts; as a friend of the keeper, the priest was acting as his accountant. At this point the search was interrupted, as an order arrived from Gardiner recalling the officers, and instructing them to leave everything as they had found it. They withdrew, leaving the priests in what amounted to a comfortable retirement in gaol.

During the Civil War Parliament needed a lodging for Royalist prisoners, but rather than lock gentlemen in with the Clink's priests, debtors and low-born villains, an order was made to requisition Winchester House as an annexe. After the war the Clink began its long final decline, as the area around it was taken over by businesses which the Great Fire had displaced from the City, often in trades such as brewing and dyeing which made them smelly objectionable neighbours. At this time the City's jurisdiction was extended to cover the prison, and sheriffs gained the power to arrest debtors within the Liberty, which must have driven away many of the area's ne'er-do-wells. Southwark's population included numbers of the sourest Puritans, and even after the Restoration it is likely that the libertine flavour had gone from the neighbourhood, and with it the supply of ruffianly prisoners for the Clink.

A census in 1732 reveals that the prison held no more than two inmates; and in the next decades the establishment moved more than once to ever more ruinous makeshift buildings, to its final site in Deadman's Place. The Gordon rioters burned the Clink down in 1780, and it was never rebuilt.

The Site Now
A plaque close to the Anchor Inn on Bankside claims to mark the site of the Clink. The plaque may stand near one of the later, temporary sites, but not to Winchester House, which was some distance to the east. The pillory, ducking-stool and cage, on the other hand, seem to have been very close to the plaque.

THE MARSHALSEA

In 1374 Edward III empowered 'the good men of Southwark to rebuild in our Royal Street which extends from the Church of the Blessed Margaret towards the South a certain House for the safe custody of the prisoners of the Marshalsea'.

The title Marshalsea derives from a rank within the Royal Household. The Lord Steward and Earl Marshal presided in an ancient court whose jurisdiction extended for twelve miles around the King's lodging, this jurisdiction moving with the King in his travels, so that members of the entourage would be subject to the King's court rather than to a local one. The gaol in Southwark was from early times used by the monarch as a state prison serving this court, the more useful for being across the river away from both Westminster and the City; for many years it ranked second only to the Tower.

Courts guard their powers jealously, and just three years after the Marshalsea prison was created a riot broke out when the Marshal imprisoned a man whom the City of London regarded as privileged. The citizens 'took armour and ran with great rage to the Marshal's Inn', broke open the gates and carried away the prisoner. In the following year the prison was attacked again, by a lynch mob of sailors incensed at the pardon granted to an esquire who had killed one of their shipmates. They pulled the man out and 'sticked him as if had been a dog'.

The Marshalsea soon acquired a reputation for the viciousness of its regime. The keeper in 1381 was described as a 'tormentor without pity', and this was one of the prisons destroyed by the Kent rebels of Wat Tyler in that year, and opened by Jack Cade's men in 1450.

The conditions in the prison provoked a great riot and breakout in 1504, and many of the recaptured men were hanged. As the building was crudely built and far from strong, escape and rescue must have been a constant problem. Furthermore, the keepers were happy to let their charges wander beyond the walls so long as a large surety had been given, or even a simple bribe.

Although the Marshalsea increasingly came to be used to hold civil debtors, it was a part of the Marshal's role to deal with any contempt of the sovereign or the royal court, which in practice meant anyone who could be regarded as defiant or mocking of authority. A notable example was the poet Christopher Brooke, imprisoned in 1609 for witnessing the secret marriage of Anne More to John Donne some eight years before. The bride had not obtained her father's permission. Donne himself had been imprisoned in the Fleet, but official pique demanded punishment for Brooke as well.

The prison grew to be a cluster of ramshackle buildings, with – as always – tolerable comfort available to the well-heeled, but with exceptional squalor for the poor and a management famously venal and sadistic. The religious conflicts of the Reformation saw both Protestants and Catholics treated brutally here, and the lowest dungeon, the Hole, was also known to Protestant prisoners as 'Bonner's Coal Hole', for the last Catholic Bishop of London, one of their oppressors. Ironically, Bonner himself was held in the Marshalsea by both Edward VI and Elizabeth, and was to die there.

A report of 1728 tells of how bad the Marshalsea had become. By this time there were more than 300 debtors confined there; and, as was the custom, the Deputy Marshal had contracted out the fees from the prison to a butcher called William Acton for £400 annual rent.

To raise this rent oppression, extortion, cruelty and even torture were exercised, the prisoners being kept in close, crowded rooms, from thirty to fifty being placed in an apartment not sixteen feet square, and three persons being allotted to each bed, each paying 2s. 6d. per week . . . When the Committee first met at the Marshalsea, in the women's ward many were found lying without beds and dying of want; and the male ward was even worse. Upon giving food to the captives with even the greatest caution, one died, his stomach having become contracted for want of use. Most of the others recovered, only nine more dying, though previously a day had seldom passed without a death, and upon the advance of spring eight or ten usually died every twenty-four hours: but though required by law, a coroner's inquest had not been for many years held in the prison.

An attempt was made to prosecute Acton for murder, but after a brief spell in gaol he was released: public outrage was strong, but did not result in any great changes.

The Marshalsea declined apace in the last years of the century. There had been changes in the law which reduced numbers but it is equally probable that the whole structure was steadily collapsing. Visiting in 1801, the reformer James Neild found only thirty-four prisoners, with eight of their wives and seven children. He remarked that the average number held a quarter of a century earlier had been 200. Loath to invest, keepers had allowed their assets to decay so far that the income could not sustain repairs. Neild reported that 'One half of it is fallen down in ruins, and the remainder in a most insecure and deplorable state.'

By 1811 the rot had gone too far, and the old prison was abandoned. A new one was built and adapted a few hundred yards away, incorporating the site of the old White Lyon Prison. Taking no account of new practices, the latest Marshalsea was again just a cluster of houses built around a courtyard and chapel. There was one concealed oddity – deep within the prison a section of the White Lyon was retained as a secure prison within a prison. The Marshalsea now held smugglers and other Excise offenders, and two cells were reserved for them. Dickens wrote of the new Marshalsea: 'Itself a close and confined prison for debtors, it contained . . . a much closer and more confined jail for smugglers . . . incarcerated behind an iron plated door, closing up a second prison, consisting of a cell or two, and a blind alley seven yards and a half wide.' In 1880, long after the premises had ceased to be a prison, the historian Walter Besant found this corner surviving exactly as Dickens had described.

Dickens was always intrigued by prisons and prisoners – his own father had been taken to the Marshalsea in 1824, and he was to make it the birthplace of Little Dorrit.

This second Marshalsea was not to last long. Although one opportunity for reform was lost when a Royal Commission of 1819 professed to find little fault with conditions in debtors' prisons, an Act of 1842 amalgamated the Marshalsea, the King's Bench and the Fleet: all their prisoners were lodged in the King's Bench (to be renamed the Queen's Bench). The Keeper of the Marshalsea (and his counterpart at the Fleet) received compensation for the closure of their profitable businesses. The prison buildings were sold, and were used for storage until demolished in 1897 during a road-widening scheme.

The Site Now
The first Marshalsea was on the east side of Borough High Street, close to the corner of Newcomen Street; the second was a little further south: the library at 211 Borough High Street covers the site. This building includes the Local Studies Library, and during the research for this book it was odd indeed to sit reading about the prison which had covered the very spot.

WHITE LYON

This was the smallest of Southwark's prisons, and from its name we can deduce that it had once been an inn, adapted to the minimal security needed to contain debtors and petty offenders. It opened in the middle years of the sixteenth century, and remained a small prison, very much in the shadow of its more important neighbours, and rarely mentioned by historians.

When other Southwark prisons became too over-crowded the White Lyon was available to receive their surplus, including religious detainees. A known example is St John Rigby, who was held for several months in 1600, before being condemned for being reconciled to the Catholic Church by a priest who had been ordained abroad – this rather contrived charge amounted to high treason under the law of the time, and Rigby was hanged, drawn and quartered.

The White Lyon faded from recorded history as unobtrusively as it had arrived. Defoe's comprehensive list of prisons standing at the beginning of the eighteenth century makes no mention of it. The assumption must be that the building decayed beyond repair and that its population was absorbed into the neighbouring gaols.

The Site Now

There is scope for detective work here. We have several bearings on the site: it was south of the early Marshalsea and King's Bench; it was just north of St George's Church; it was just back from Borough High Street, behind a tavern called the Black Bull. All this seems to place the site midway between Mermaid Court and Angle Place, between the High Street and Tennis Street.

THE BOROUGH COMPTER

The Borough Compter never rose to the national importance of its neighbouring prisons in Southwark. It was simply the local gaol, and none of its three successive buildings gained the sinister glamour attached to more famous places of punishment.

The first gaol, also known as the Clink Compter, opened around 1630. Despite its title, this was not a part of the Clink prison, but took its name from the Clink Liberty in which it stood, as a portion of the parish church of St Margaret which also held the courthouse. It was conventionally divided into Master's and Common Sides, but more interesting was the management imposed upon it. The City was always eager to control the loose life of Southwark, and although the bailiff of the Clink Liberty was able to nominate keepers of the Borough Compter, power of appointment was vested in the City's Court of Aldermen.

By 1714 the compter had moved, to become a part of the Marshalsea, a corner of the larger prison's sprawl. The traditional abuses continued, and in 1756 the Lord Mayor chose the occasion of the election of a new bailiff to comment on the extortion of fees from compter prisoners. He was addressing the Court of Common Council, which immediately passed a motion forbidding the taking of fees from offenders. Debtors, it may be conjectured, would instead be called upon to make up the shortage in the keeper's income.

We know that the Thames rose unusually high in 1762, to flood the compter's yard, with imaginable consequences for prisoners held at ground level or below. The compter moved again in 1787, to a new building in Mill Lane, by Tooley Street, probably because the Marshalsea was so dilapidated.

The new building was small, having only five debtor inmates when Neild visited in 1802. Accommodation was nonetheless cramped: the debtors shared just two rooms, six cells were provided for offenders, and there was a holding cell for overnight arrests. Of the debtors' side Neild wrote:

The debtors have only one small courtyard, about nineteen feet square . . . No bedding, or even straw to lie upon. No mops, brooms, or pails, to keep the prison clean. No fire in the winter; the casements rotting off their hinges, and scarce a whole pane of glass in the windows of the women's side . . . The men debtors' room below stairs totally in ruins, having but four or five boards upon it, and those in a rotten decayed state.

The prison received charitable bequests and gifts, but no care was taken in their administration. A gift of sixty-five penny loaves arrived every eight weeks 'all at one time, so that if there is but one prisoner he has the whole, and sells them. The donation of twenty shillings by the Archbishop of Canterbury each Christmas is distributed in the same manner.'

There were better rooms available for rent, it seems, but no takers. The Borough Compter seems to have taken the poorest of debtors, the better-off lodging in more fashionable gaols. The Borough Compter closed in 1855, and the remaining prisoners went to the newly re-named Queen's Bench.

The Site Now
The site of the first compter is now marked by the war memorial on the island in Borough High Street which holds branches of the National Westminster and Midland banks. The second was at the Marshalsea, and the third some distance away, where Jamaica Road now begins, on the downstream side of the Neckinger inlet.

MYNSHUL

Geffray Mynshul was imprisoned in the King's Bench for debt, and in 1617 wrote *Certaine Characters and Essayes of Prison and Prisoners*, a perfectly eloquent tale of the debtor's plight.

A Prison is a grave to bury men alive, and a place wherein a man for half a year's imprisonment may learne more lawe, than he can at Westminster for a hundred pound.

It is a Microcosmos, a little world of woe, it is a mappe of misery, it is a place that will learn a young man more villainy if he be apt to take it in one half yeare, than he can learn at twenty dyeing houses, Bowling allyes, Brothel houses, or Ordinaryes, and an old man more policie than if he had bin a pupil to Machiavil.

It is a place that hath more diseases predominant in it, than the pest-house in the plague-tyme, and it stinckes more than the Lord Mayor's doggehouse or paris-garden in August.

A Prisoner is an impatient patient lingring under the rough hands of a cruel physition, his creditour having cast his water knoes his disease and hath power to cure him, but takes more pleasure to kill him.

A Jaylor is as Cruell to his prisoners as a dogge-killer in the plague time to a diseased curre, and shewes no more pity to a young Gentleman than the unconscionable Citizen that laid him in: when they meete you in the streetes they shewe themselves more humble to you than a whore when she is brought before a Constable or a Cheater before a Justice, but when you fall into their fingers, they will be as currish as they seemed kind.

They are like Bawdes and Beadles, that live upon the sins of the people, mens foillies fill their purses.

KING'S BENCH

Like the Marshalsea, this was a prison which took its name from the court it served. The court was originally mobile, travelling with the king's household, and in 1331 the Marshals were given the power to detain prisoners in houses in assigned towns. Fifty years later the prison had become a fixed establishment on the east side of Borough High Street in Southwark, where it was attacked and burned by the rebels of 1381 and 1450.

This prison seems to have had few distinguishing characteristics except for the small size of its rooms. It became a busy debtors' prison, and in the sixteenth century there were complaints that the cramped quarters were causing illness and death – it cannot have helped that the prison stood on low and marshy ground. This was among the prisons used to hold religious–political prisoners during the swings of persecution, and from it both Protestant and Catholic martyrs went to their deaths. Among them, the Blessed John Pibush was remarkable; convicted of treason in 1595 he was first held among the common criminals, and was rejected and obstructed by them in his attempts to pray and receive visits from friends, but in time he won their respect, was given the use of a separate small garret, and even allowed to celebrate Mass. Accused of making converts to the Catholic Church, he went to the scaffold at St Thomas Waterings in 1600.

The prison moved to the west of the High Street, and one of the prisoners to make the move from the old prison to the new was Theodore, King of Corsica, who was committed for debt in 1752, and died shortly after his release in 1766, having registered his kingdom for the benefit of his creditors. The new prison was vast, with 224 rooms, but by all accounts cheerless. It seems to have been internally partitioned with timber to create cubicles –

there is mention of a secure room built of stone, and brick reinforcement installed only after a fire. There were many taprooms serving beer and gin, and the entertainments included a game called 'bumble-puppy grounds' – players tossed small iron balls at a frame with holes, to achieve the highest score – and more enduring sports such as rackets and fives.

In 1770 a mob attacked the prison, intending to carry a prisoner called John Wilkes to the House of Commons. Wilkes was a demagogic politician who pleased the people by his passionate concern for freedom, but infuriated the conventional establishment, who regarded him as 'a blasphemer of his God and libeller of his King', and although elected to Parliament he was barred from the House. The mob refused to disperse, soldiers opened fire, and many were killed or injured in what came to be known as the St George's Field Massacre. Wilkes went on to be an enormously popular Lord Mayor of London, and took a major part in preserving London from even greater destruction in the anti-Catholic Gordon Riots of 1780. Ironically, he was unable to save the King's Bench, which was burned.

The prison was hastily rebuilt. It became doubly notorious for the privilege it offered the wealthy – 'the most desirable place of incarceration in London' – and the conditions in which the poor were kept, which rivalled 'the purlieus of Wapping, St Giles and St James' in vice, debauchery and drunkenness'. It was similar to the Fleet in having a broad area of Rules in which the better-off could take comfortable lodgings, and in permitting prisoners to pursue a very wide range of trades and callings within the prison itself.

In 1842 the name was changed to the Queen's Bench (during the rule of Parliament and Cromwell it had briefly been called the Upper Bench), and prisoners were received from the Fleet and Marshalsea in an amalgamation to provide for the smaller numbers of debtors. Further changes in the law came close to abolishing imprisonment for debt, and the Queen's Bench was handed over for use as a military prison, having lost 'the buffoonery, scoundrelism, riot and confusion which had formerly made it picturesque'. It was demolished in 1880.

The Site Now
The original King's Bench stood between Borough High Street and Tennis Street, on the south side of Mermaid Court. The later, post-1758 prison was at the eastern end of Borough Road close to the High Street. That site, opposite the Inner London Crown Court, is within the modern Scovill Estate.

IMPRISONMENT FOR DEBT

It seems likely that from the fourteenth to nineteenth centuries at least as many Londoners were locked up for debt as for crime, and it certainly must have been the case that with the exception of a very few state prisoners, debtors spent longer behind bars than the most serious offenders.

To send a debtor to prison was intended in the first instance to coerce him into payment, in effect to hold him hostage until settlement was made. This was a power taken in the twelfth century by kings who wished to collect from Crown debtors, and was as much a matter of preserving royal dignity and suppressing corruption, or punishing incompetence, as a simple demand for cash. Only very slowly did the practice extend to other debts, and still the emphasis was on seizing those who owed not only money but a duty, such as a steward who lined his own pockets or squandered money entrusted to him. A Statute of Merchants in 1285 made it possible for important merchants to register major debts and use imprisonment to enforce them, but this still fell far short of what was to follow. These earlier laws also made the creditor responsible for feeding the debtor if he could not support himself.

In 1352 a brief and ill-considered passage in a much larger statute extended the use of immediate imprisonment to civil debt in general, and began a practice that would cause appalling misery for centuries to come.

It was now possible for a creditor to obtain a warrant committing the debtor immediately to gaol, and the original purpose was the honourable one of providing a means, when ordinary social pressures had failed, for a creditor to obtain satisfaction. What happened instead was a legal catastrophe which did little to defend traders, and placed more debtors behind bars than criminals; and to understand the reasons we must look not at the law but at the system which grew around it.

Modern debt collectors make a living by the commission that they charge on the original debt, but the officers who enforced the old laws derived most of their income from the fees which they were able to collect, and in this lay the source of the problem.

If a creditor swore out a warrant against a debtor, he paid a fee to the prison sergeant or other officer. The officer might then take a fee from the debtor *not* to enforce it, and play the two parties off for quite a time. The official fee for enforcement was one shilling, but most sergeants would not contemplate accepting one unless paid much more.

If the debtor were arrested, a further round of fee-taking began. The prisons were foul, and an alternative could be arranged, to pay the officer for lodging in the officer's own house, or in rented rooms which he had taken – this was expensive. If the debtor could not afford this option, he would be taken to a gaol, and start to pay fees there. If he or his family could raise the cash to bring him out of prison, both the creditor and the gaolers would have done well. If he could not afford to leave, he would continue to pay fees for as long as he remained behind bars, or live very poorly on charity.

This system offered a number of possibilities for the greedy. Sergeants actively sought out creditors, and urged them to swear out warrants for a slice of the fees; young men of good family might be tempted into debt so that their wealthy parents would pay well to rescue them from gaol. At a lower social level the tallymen flourished – like similar operators today they induced citizens to buy goods on credit, gave poor value but demanded extortionate interest, while keeping a working agreement with the local officers which guaranteed a kickback of gaol fees from the defaulters. At worst, the debtor might not even have bought tangible goods, but been foolish enough to promise investment in a speculative scheme which was never intended to bear fruit.

The foulest sections of the prisons were filled with poor debtors who would/could spend most of a lifetime there, but in the more expensive parts, or out in the Liberties of the Fleet or the King's Bench, were the 'Politic Debtors'. These were wealthy and wily men who had deliberately or recklessly run up debts with no intention of paying. They took the decision to live well in prison rather than in poverty outside, and might spend many years in gaol, not least because they knew that under the laws of the time their debts would die with them. A survey of the Upper (King's) Bench prisoners in 1653 showed that only thirty-eight of the debtors owed less than £100, and the average amount was £2,500; in such cases the creditor had gained nothing by his warrant, and often had to seek a settlement for much less than the true debt.

To remove the debtors from prison required the development of new remedies for creditors and new defences for debtors, and was a process which lasted from 1813 to 1970. A court was created to deal with insolvent debtors, to hear the circumstances of individual cases; the 1844 Insolvency Act abolished imprisonment for debts below £20, and allowed private persons to go into bankruptcy, which had previously been reserved for traders. Further Acts in the 1840s and 1850s progressively lowered the numbers held in prison, and in 1861 registrars of courts of bankruptcy were authorized to go into gaols and, if satisfied that there was real insolvency, to order the release of the prisoner. In 1869 the Act for the Abolition of Imprisonment for Debt was passed, but failed to live up to its name: to default on a payment would not in itself lead to imprisonment, but if a debtor had the means to pay, yet neglected or refused to pay, he or she could be locked up for six weeks. This provision lasted until the 1960s, when there were still more than 60,000 people committed to prison each year.

Since 1970 the position has been restored to what it had been 800 years ago – apart from maintenance defaulters, the only people who can be imprisoned are those owing money to the Crown.

As in the Fleet, those who wished to remain prosperous by taking shelter from their creditors could live well within the King's Bench.

HORSEMONGER LANE GAOL

Horsemonger Lane was the address, and the common name of the Surrey County Gaol built in Southwark in 1791 to 1779 as a replacement for the older Southwark prisons, particularly the White Lyon. A new Sessions House – courthouse – was a part of the same scheme, but faced on to Newington Causeway.

Behind a squat, broad gatehouse was a three-storey quadrangle with three wings for petty criminals and a fourth for debtors. The gatehouse was made even more sinister by the gallows which was erected on the roof for the execution of Surrey's felons. In 1803 Colonel Despard, who had conceived a wild plot to assassinate the King and seize the Tower and the Bank of England, was hanged here, but history remembers better the hanging of Mr and Mrs Manning, who had killed their lodger, in 1849, which prompted Charles Dickens to write to *The Times*:

I do not believe that any community can prosper where such a scene of horror as was enacted this morning outside Horsemonger Lane gaol is permitted. The horrors of the gibbet and of the crime which brought the wretched murderers to it faded in my mind before the atrocious looks and language of the assembled spectators.

The letter contributed to the eventual abolition of public hanging. Another effect of the execution was the immediate plunge from favour of the style of black dress worn by Mrs Manning on the scaffold.

The prison seems to have been unadorned but better than many. Neild found in 1800 that there were two surgeons who attended the prison, and commented on the cleanliness and good order of 'this excellently well-regulated gaol', and some fifty years later it made a fair impression on Mayhew's colleague John Binny. Closed in 1878 after being taken over by the Prison Commissioners, Horsemonger Lane had served modestly but well. The design of Horsemonger Lane has been identified as the model for Roscommon Jail in Ireland. Roscommon was built in 1818, and also incorporated a courthouse, but lasted rather longer than the Surrey original, its last portion demolished as late as 1945.

The Site Now

In this cramped inner city area the borough chose to use the site, on the south side of Harper Road east of Newington Causeway, as a public garden and playground. The history of the site has not been forgotten, and generations of local children have been sent by their parents to play at 'The Gaol'.

LAMBETH PALACE

Since the end of the twelfth century the official residence of the Archbishop of Canterbury has been Lambeth Palace, across the river from Westminster Abbey. Like other church properties, Lambeth must have held clerical offenders, and we have evidence of individuals who were detained here, including the Earl of Essex, Elizabeth's fallen favourite, who was committed to the palace before being taken to the Tower.

Within the palace is a tower, built in 1435 to contain a water supply, which has become known as the Lollards' Tower, and reputed to have been a prison in which Lollard heretics were incarcerated. There is certainly a prison on an upper floor, with a heavy oaken lining and iron rings set into the walls, but it is almost certainly a seventeenth-century adaptation, carried out 200 years too late to have held any Lollards. It is possible that there was a previous tower on the site which first carried the name, and that it was carried over to the later building. Other possible explanations can be drawn from the history of the Church's treatment of medieval dissent: in 1378 Wycliffe was examined at length at Lambeth because his puritanical preaching offended the Church, and his belief that the Church should return to poverty and simplicity was carried over into the Lollard movement of the next century. There was an authentic Lollards' Tower, but it was on the south side of the old St Paul's Cathedral in the City, and heretics were certainly held, tortured and killed there. The cathedral was destroyed in the Great Fire, at about the time that the Lambeth tower became a prison; perhaps the title was unwittingly transferred by later generations.

CAGES, LOCK-UPS AND SPONGING-HOUSES

Throughout London were small local places of detention which served the same purpose as the police station cells of today: overnight drunks sobered up in them, and brawlers regained their composure before being shown the door in the morning. Those whose behaviour was a little worse would make their way next day to a local court for summary trial, but those who had committed serious offences would soon be moved to a grander, more secure prison.

These local lock-ups and cages were built and maintained by parishes, to varying patterns. Some were separate constructions, cages of timber, or brick and stone buildings varying in size from a bus-stop shelter to a domestic double garage; a design commonly used was the roundhouse, a simple and strong shape. Others formed a part of another public building such as a courthouse, town hall, or the local manor house. When a district had a watchman, before the creation of the police force, the lock-up was commonly combined with the watchhouse. Stocks or a gibbet, or both, might stand nearby, especially if the lock-up occupied a prominent position. Lock-ups were commonly close to an important crossroads, as in Camden Town, or by a local landmark such as a church; a lock-up stood opposite St Martin-in-the-Fields for many years.

These lock-ups were all publicly owned buildings intended to hold offenders, but there were also local private lodgings where debtors were held. Sponging-houses were used by bailiffs to detain anyone whose creditor had gone to law, sometimes as a preliminary to delivering the debtor to a prison. It must often have been the case that a debtor would feel intimidated by arrest and detention, and pay up. Equally it was possible for a debtor to choose to be taken to a sponging-house as an alternative to imprisonment, and live in comparative comfort, though of course paying rent to the bailiff, whose own home would usually serve for the detention. Defoe reported that there were 109 sponging-houses in London at the beginning of the eighteenth century.

The houses of some public officials were also legitimate places to hold prisoners: King's Messengers, Admiralty and Chancery Officers, and officers of Black Rod and the Sergeant at Arms each added to Defoe's list of 'tolerated prisons' as these small profitable establishments were known.

TRANSPORTATION

To remove an offender from society you can kill him, lock him away, or – to take an alternative no longer possible for British courts – send him beyond your frontiers. He will then pose no further threat, and will be sharply punished by the loss of the property and companionship he leaves behind.

Banishment is an ancient punishment, and was often an implicit sentence of death, since a lone traveller would be unwelcome elsewhere and quite likely to perish. In Anglo-Saxon times, outlawry placed a man outside his society, his property was forfeit, and law-abiding people were expected to enforce the sanction by hunting to death any outlaw, in a kind of lay excommunication. Technical changes were made by Magna Carta, which specified that no freeman should be outlawed except by lawful judgement, never again merely at the whim of the monarch. Extraordinarily, the penalty of outlawry was not legally abolished until 1938, although civil outlawry, by which anyone who absconded before a civil case was heard was liable to forfeit property, had ended in 1879.

Less drastic than outlawry was exile, or banishment. Those who sought Sanctuary were expected to quit the realm. This process had been abolished for only a generation when the first statute authorizing banishment as a sentence of the court was passed in 1579, at first only as a penalty for vagabondage, but later extended to petty criminals and Quakers. The Act also provided for service in the galleys – even plans for a galley fleet – but perhaps this was too great a departure from naval tradition, which preferred sail to manpower.

Throughout the seventeenth century increasing use was made of transportation as governments discovered how useful a disposal it could be. Certain religious offenders had previously been allowed to leave the realm as an alternative to execution, and it was swiftly appreciated that systematic transportation of these troublesome prisoners would stifle the dissidents as effectively as death, and would prevent their attaining the status of martyrs. Catholics, extreme Protestants, and by a logical extension rebellious Scots were all banished, on ships bound for Barbados, Virginia and the East Indies. The sentence was not simply exile: on arrival in the colonies the prisoners were put to hard labour, slaves indentured to their masters.

The system seemed very satisfactory to the lawmakers. Transportation was less morally objectionable than hanging, which had become the statutory penalty for so many minor offences; if many of the convicts died in shipwrecks, of the privations of the voyage or the hardships overseas, this was the hand of Fate or the will of God rather than deliberate execution. The economic arguments persuaded many – here was a scheme which was much cheaper than imprisonment at home, and provided a workforce for profitable exploitation of the colonies.

It was time to apply this new approach to criminals in general, and it was provided that courts might transport for periods of seven and fourteen years. Since this was often an alternative to hanging, objections from defendants were few, and there were some who seemed to have deliberately brought transportation upon themselves as offering a way out of their wretched lives in Britain.

Virginia and Maryland were the favoured destinations, and prisoners were carried there by contractors who at first received a flat fee, but later at no charge. Instead of the flat fee of £5 a head, one contractor sold his cargoes according to their strength and skills – for women he received £8, for unskilled men £10, for craftsmen between £15 and £25, against which he had to pay 'humane personages' to take away the aged and disabled convicts.

The American War of Independence brought a sudden end to this traffic. By an Act of 1776 a hurried alternative to transportation was created; for a limited period courts would be able to pass sentences of three to ten years' hard labour on men who would otherwise have been transported. This was the beginning of the hulk system, as men used in public works were confined at night to floating gaols. Like transportation, the hulks were not operated by the state, but delegated to a private contractor, a certain Duncan Campbell, who had previously shipped convicts to America. The interruption of transportation also gave impetus to the development of a penitentiary, leading eventually to the building of Millbank and Pentonville.

Governments were reluctant to discard transportation, and other possible destinations were considered. Africa was ruled out, but Australia seemed promising, with a high demand for labour of all kinds. In 1787 the First Fleet set off. It consisted of nine transports escorted by two warships, and reached New South Wales in January of the following year, after a journey even more hazardous than the Atlantic crossing. Those first prisoners, whose arrival is celebrated as marking the birth of modern Australia, had fared quite well, but of 983 prisoners who embarked two years later, 273 died en route and a further 486 were seriously ill on arrival.

Transportation began again, and for even greater numbers of prisoners. At the beginning of the eighteenth

century only 5,000 had been sent abroad; now an equal
number was leaving Britain each year. Most went to
Australia, but some were shipped to hulks in Gibraltar
and Bermuda, and in one failed attempt, to the Cape of
Good Hope.

At Millbank and Pentonville convicts were assessed, and
prepared for their life abroad in a systematic way, and
prisoners left Britain already classified for the work and
the degree of liberty which they would be permitted in the
colonies. Within a generation enthusiasm for the system
waned in Australia and at home: convicts did not make
the best settlers, and eventually Western Australia had a
demand for raw labour, while in Britain the emphasis
had shifted to the virtues of reform rather than exile.
The greatest obstacle to keeping prisoners in Britain
was the shortage of suitable prison accommodation, but
by the 1850s an alternative sentence – penal servitude,
shorter periods of hard labour at home – was created,
and transportation was brought to an end. The need to
cope with a much larger prison population led not only
to a major programme of building new prisons, but to the
centralization of prison control.

In 1851, just as Britain was abandoning transportation,
the French began to use it, creating among other penal
colonies the most famous of them all – Devil's Island.

The Site Now

One spot in London is firmly associated with transportation. On Millbank, close to the Tate Gallery, is a
plaque marking the point from which thousands left
the penitentiary to journey around the world. Close by,
in a courtyard of the Royal Army Medical College, are
bollards once used to moor the boats which carried the
convicts.

THE HULKS

When the American War of Independence prevented the transportation of any more convicts to the New World, the prisons faced one of the many overcrowding problems in their history. The idea of using redundant ships as floating accommodation was put forward, and just as convicts had worked in the colonies, so they could now provide manpower for public works in England. The 1776 Act declared:

> For the more severe and effectual punishment of atrocious and daring offenders . . . where any Male Person . . . shall be liable by Law to be transported . . . it shall and may be lawful for the Court to order and adjudge that such Person . . . shall be punished by being kept on Board Ships or Vessels properly accommodated for the Security, Employment and Health of the Persons to be confined therein, and by being employed in Hard Labour in the raising Sand, Soil and Gravel from, and cleansing the River Thames . . .

The wars with France between 1793 and 1815 interrupted further transportation, provided some prize ships which could be used, and made obsolete vessels available. The hulks were to be a two-year temporary expedient, but lasted until 1859 in England, and until 1875 in Gibraltar.

The management of the first hulks was contracted to an overseer with experience of transportation. He received

£38 per annum per prisoner, for which he supplied,
equipped and staffed the two first vessels, and fed, clothed
and disciplined the convicts. He had no stake in the
prisoners' work, which was for government projects, and
the Home Department had overall supervision and took
responsibility for discharges and gratuities. Transported
convicts had been given money with which to start a new
life, and a man held in the hulks had the same privilege,
taking some of his cash on discharge, and the remainder
some months later if he could secure the signature of a
clergyman or other respectable citizen on a form letter
attesting to his honest life. Allowing for inflation, these
grants were more generous than those given to discharged
prisoners in the 1980s.

Sadly, many of the convicts did not live to receive
their gratuities: some years there were more deaths than
discharges. Of 632 prisoners taken on board the *Justitia*
between August 1776 and March 1778, 176 died. Even
after years of criticism and promises of change, the surgeon
on one ship, the *Warrior*, reported 400 admissions to
hospital, and 38 deaths, among the 638 prisoners on
board.

Conditions on board were notoriously cramped and
foul, with little supervision – the 700 prisoners on the
Justitia were simply locked in overnight in the charge of
a single warder!

The hulks formed a strange waterborne community.
The first ships were moored between Gallions Reach and
Barking Reach to tackle cleansing work, but soon the
major task began of building the docks for the Royal
Arsenal at Woolwich. At any one time there would be
half a dozen ships, including at one time the *Discovery*
which had been one of the ships in Captain Cook's last
expedition. The ships were an odd mixture of whatever
became available: the *Warrior* and the *Defence* were ancient

*Prisoners in the Fleet
supported themselves
by begging through a
grille which gave on
to Farringdon Street.*

LEFT: *Fleet Prison, with its begging grate just visible behind the lamp standard on the right.*

BELOW LEFT: *One of the drink shops within the Fleet.*

BELOW: *Bridewell Palace retained a nobility of appearance but the stocks in the nearer courtyard betray the change of use.*

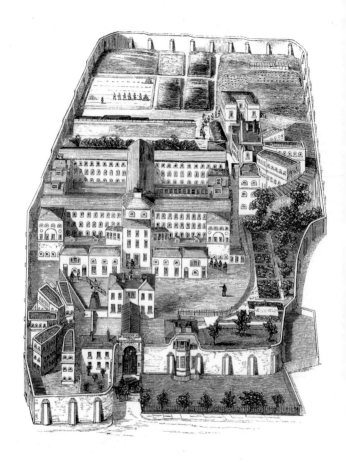

*Ideas about prison design
changed during the expansion of
Coldbath Fields, and this view
from the 1850s shows something
of the chaos. To the left of the
first house beyond the gate are
the horizontal blades turned by
the treadmill.*

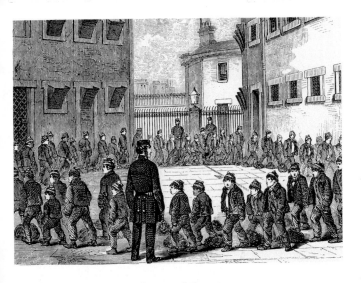

*Watching boys such as these trudging at
Tothill Fields, Mayhew could tell 'how little
used many of them had been to such a luxury
as shoe leather'.*

*The immensity of Millbank Penitentiary
is plain in this view from the riverside.
Between roadside fence and the prison
wall was a moat.*

*This view of Marshalsea
from 1773 shows how any
group of buildings might serve
as a prison – the rooms had
fanciful names such as
Sportsman's Hall, Belle Isle,
and Nova Scotia.*

TEN POUNDS REWARD.

Escaped

From the Borough Compter, Southwark, on Monday Morning, December 3, 1827, between the Hours of 12 and 3 o'Clock, CATHERINE GALLOWAY, otherwise SULLIVAN, otherwise MOORE, 31 years of age, about 5 feet 6 inches high, rather dark red hair, light grey eyes, sallowish complexion, long visage; had on when she went away a dark brown stuff gown, trimmed with red braid, an old chocolate silk handkerchief, white apron with pink flowers, white stockings, and an old light cotton shawl; also an old pair of leather shoes, the hind quarters tied over the instep with black tape.

The aforesaid is a native of Ireland, and has latterly been employed in carrying milk, and occasionally as a Basket Woman in and about the Borough Market and Billingsgate.

Whoever will apprehend and lodge her in any of His Majesty's Gaols, shall receive the above Reward by applying to the Keeper of the aforesaid Prison.

Borough Compter, Mill Lane,
Tooley Street, December 3, 1827.

Security in the Borough Compter was as poor as in other minor gaols. The good size of the reward offered here probably reflected the Keeper's fear for his job rather than the seriousness of Ms Galloway's crimes.

74-gunners, holding 450 and 520 men. The *Unite*, moored to *Defence*, was a 36-gun frigate that had been taken from the French and used as a hospital ship for up to 60 men. The 30-gun sloop *Sulphur* was a laundry on which fifteen men worked, but lodged no prisoners.

The features which we associate with nineteenth-century prisons were also found in the regime on board the hulks, though the crowding and decay were remarkable even for the time. Chapel attendance and schooling were the norm offshore as on land, but the work was harder. Labour on land may have been pointless and taxing, but for the hulk gangs stone-breaking was regarded as undemanding work suitable for invalids. Taken ashore under armed guard, the men worked without the incentives given to transported men. In the colonies men were given increasing freedom and the prospect of a fresh start, but on the hulks, the danger of escape so close to London meant that the men were ringed with carbines, bayonets fixed. Some inevitably did get away, but few.

The prisoners were supposed to be the most hardened, serious offenders yet they included boys under ten years of age. The weak were at the mercy of the tough once the ships had been battened down for the night. The work was back-breaking and the wards infested. Minimal concern was shown by the staff: when cholera swept through the ships, and the dead had been taken ashore, the chaplain conducted the burial service from a full mile away on the poop of his ship, signalling with his handkerchief that the bodies be lowered.

Not surprisingly, there was indiscipline of every kind. At worst, there were mutinies and there were persistent rackets and dodges, including a coin-forging operation. It must have been particularly galling for the hulk convicts to know that the prisons on shore were becoming even healthier and better-run, while their conditions worsened on poorly-maintained wooden ships up to sixty years old.

In 1859 the convict prisons and hulks were brought under the control of central government, but they were not to last much longer. In 1857 the *Defence* caught fire and had to be scuttled. It had been the last of the large hulks, and when its prisoners were taken to Millbank, only the invalids aboard the *Unite* remained. In haste, the old county gaol at Lewes which had been bought by the Government, and was in use by the Admiralty, was leased to become an invalid convict prison, and the last prisoners left the river.

The Site Now
The hulks were moored just upstream of the Thames Barrier. At the time of writing, planning has reached an advanced stage for the latest London prison to be built at Woolwich close to where the hulk convicts worked.

VICTORIAN
DEVELOPMENTS

INTRODUCTION

Of the five large prisons in London today, four were built
in the nineteenth century, and all of these will remain in
use well past the year 2000. When we think of prisons,
we have in our minds the tall, galleried wings lined with
small cells characteristic of Victorian prison design, the
imposing gatehouses with massive studded doors set in
tall brick walls which surround them.

The ancient prisons of London did not follow this
pattern, nor do the new establishments of our time. Every
feature can be seen as arising from an aspect of Victorian
life and thought.

The location of Victorian prisons gives us the first signs.
London was expanding rapidly, with a population that
grew during the nineteenth century from about one million
people to well over six million. To find sites which could
accommodate the much larger prisons needed, planners
had to look for less expensive land well beyond the City,
Southwark and Westminster. They were also concerned to
place prisons in healthy settings where disease would not
threaten the prisoners, and placed great faith in sites with
clean open surroundings well beyond the sulphurous fogs
of the town, and the problems of transporting prisoners

greater distances from the centre were solved with the construction of the railways.

On their new sites the Victorians did not build discreetly. The restrained elegance of the Georgians was now rejected as bad taste, and the new prisons must in their outward appearance be impressive representatives of the new bold and elaborate fashions. Public buildings, whether town halls, libraries or prisons were expected to reflect the ambitious spirit of the age. The size of the prisons was not merely a practical matter – it would have been possible to build a larger number of smaller gaols – but spoke of the century's belief in grand solutions. Vast workhouses had replaced little rows of almshouses, the citizens travelled between enormous railway stations rather than coaching inns – everywhere stood evidence that bigger was better.

Within the prisons were structures which demonstrated another aspect of Victorian belief. Older prisons had accommodated prisoners in large wards, dormitories for dozens. This was quite unacceptable to the new designers: there was now some understanding of the causes of disease and the need for hygiene, and it was clear that risks of infection would be improved if wards were replaced by smaller units. But prisoners' safety and comfort was only a secondary concern – prisons were now intended not only to contain but to reform, and individual confinement would be the means of saving criminals.

This was an age of optimism in which there seemed always to be a practical solution to every problem. Theorists at the beginning of the nineteenth century believed that they had found that answer to criminality in a form of imprisonment in which there would be total separation of prisoners from each other – they would have no opportunity to talk, conspire, or corrupt each other, but would each be isolated and obliged to contemplate their wicked ways. Hard work and education would combine

with firm spiritual guidance to turn them to the paths of
righteousness, and to achieve this prisoners would each
have a cell, cut off from all others, in which to seek their
salvation.

The prisons which this philosophy produced are now
dismissed as warehouses for humans. Two, three and four
men at a time are now lodged in those individual cells; the
lack of decent sanitation, of areas in which prisoners may
mingle socially, and the desperate difficulty of maintaining
such old structures while retaining the capacity and the
security demanded, have turned these reformers' ideal
designs into shameful penal slums. Worse, those reforming
ideas never did have any substance. The story of London's
Victorian prisons is one of perpetual failure.

BRIXTON

Brixton is the oldest of London's gaols still receiving
prisoners, for as long as the Tower remains no more
than a tourist attraction.

When the prison was built, the old grim Fleet, Newgate
and Marshalsea prisons were still in use, and Brixton
village was at the agricultural fringe of the capital. The
Surrey Justices decided to build a new House of Correction
and in 1819 accepted a design by Thomas Chawner the
county surveyor which promised better lodging for short-
term prisoners. It was built 'in the form of a rude crescent,
the governor's house being in the common centre, and his
drawing-room window commanding a view of all the
yards'.

With a healthy location and individual cells Brixton
should have been a change for the better, but there were
problems even before the prison was complete. When
the outer wall and gatehouse were up a work party

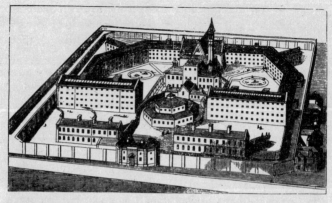

The police helicopter which today circles Brixton during the transfer of important prisoners looks down on much the same collection of buildings as the artist of one hundred and thirty years ago.

of twenty-five prisoners was brought in to help in the construction. Before long, three of them had escaped, and the governor was dismissed.

Much more seriously, the accommodation in the new gaol was in every sense too small. Each of the individual cells measured only 8 feet by 7 feet 6 inches by 6 feet, and was poorly ventilated. Built to hold 175 prisoners, Brixton was soon taking 400. There was a law intended to prevent overcrowding, which forbade two prisoners to be held in one cell; however, that law said nothing about confining *three* together, so that is how they were housed (with bedding for just two). This resulted, not just in discomfort, but also in the very danger to health which the new prison was intended to prevent. In a single year, in which 4,043 prisoners passed through, there were 1,085 reported cases of sickness, including 249 of fever.

As a house of correction Brixton put its prisoners to work. It was the first English prison to use a treadwheel, a vast drum with slatted steps on which a line of prisoners would pace, turning a shaft which at Brixton was connected to a millhouse in which corn was ground. (Not every wheel served a useful purpose – *see* Coldbath Fields.)

The treadwheel was an idea that had come to William Cubitt, a civil engineer, a couple of years previously during a visit to the gaol in Bury St Edmunds. A magistrate showing Cubitt around had waved an arm at a group of lounging prisoners and lamented: 'I wish to God, Mr Cubitt, you could suggest to us some mode of employing these fellows! Could nothing like a wheel become available?' Cubitt's inspired response was 'The wheel elongated!' The enterprising Surrey Justices were his first customers, paying £6,913 3s. 6d. for their mill. The wheel was a great novelty to the public. It was the subject of poems and featured as a stage prop in a production called *The Tread Mill*, or *Tom and Jerry at Brixton*, described as 'A serio, comic, operatic, milldramatic farcical moral Burletta in two acts as performed originally at The Surrey Theatre and received with unanimous applause'. One piece of business in the performance was a racy scene in which the stage treadwheel 'takes old Pringle by the skirts, tears them off'.

By the mid-1840s the Surrey magistrates wanted to make a fresh start. After an assessment of probable future needs, they decided to rationalize their operations, and decided to close not only Brixton, but also their other prisons at Kingston and Guildford, concentrating all the prisoners in a single larger House of Correction. This was to be Wandsworth.

Brixton was offered for sale to central government. Its use as a lunatic asylum was discussed, but nothing came of the negotiations, and in September 1852 the prison was sold at auction to Sir William Tite, developer and architect of the Norwood Cemetery. He paid £8,450, expecting to demolish the prison and turn a profit on the materials. We must assume that Surrey was eager to be rid of the place – they had paid £51,780 17s. 7d. for the building (including the treadwheel) thirty-three years before.

Central government expressed further interest at this point, and, after bureaucratic delays which took Tite to the point of setting an auction date for the fabric of the gaol, Brixton was sold to the Prison Commissioners in May 1853 for £13,000.

The Commissioners' first step was to extend its new property. Fortunately, provision had been made from the first for expansion 'should the increasing depravity of the Lower Orders subject the County to that burthensome obligation'. A further wing was added to each end of the original crescent, and a new chapel, laundry, and houses for the superintendent and chaplain were built.

The expanded Brixton was the first exclusively female convict prison. Transportation was slowing down, and would soon end, creating a need for a large prison at home. Brixton was not only expanded but had also been adapted to take its new charges. The treadwheel was removed, and the new laundry was intended to provide suitable work for women – they would take in washing from other prisons. A nursery was created, and a uniform – of spotted blue material – designed for the prison's infants.

This was to be a women's prison, run by women. In 1856 there was a staff of sixty-five, of whom only seventeen were men, employed mainly on maintenance work in trades such as carpentry and plumbing. The chaplain was a man, as was the surgeon, but overall command – with the title of 'superintendent' rather than 'governor' – was in the hands of Mrs Emma Martin.

By any standards Mrs Martin was a remarkable woman. Twice widowed, she came to the work because her second husband had been chaplain to the convict establishment at Woolwich. When she took up her appointment she had twelve children, of whom eleven – aged between six months and seventeen years – survived. Businesslike but kindly, she took her own small children into the prison so that they could play and remain close to her. When Mayhew visited the prison Mrs Martin made a great impression, both by her own responses, and by the standards of care and kindliness she set for her staff.

Sadly, much of the goodwill in Brixton was lost after changes in national policy. Long sentences of transportation had meant a short period in prison followed by comparative liberty once Australia was reached.

The substitution of long sentences behind bars in England was the end of hope for many. There were disturbances, attacks on officers, and a grave loss of morale. The national system was evolving; one decision led to the transfer of Brixton's prisoners to Holloway, and Brixton was converted to a military prison. In 1897 it was returned to the Prison Commissioners, who used money raised by the sale of the Newgate site to the City to create a new remand prison for the London area. Brixton also held short-term prisoners, and we have accounts of the conditions there for prisoners in the First (more comfortable) Division. One author went so far as to call his memoir *A Holiday In Gaol*. Bertrand Russell, sentenced for writing a pamphlet which the wartime government disliked, compared his time there to sailing aboard an ocean liner, with days spent promenading before retiring to a cabin. The privileges of the First Division included being able to hire other prisoners to act almost as servants, and the right to follow a trade or profession. Russell found it easy to write, since he 'had no engagements, no difficult decisions to make, no fear of callers, no interruptions to my work'. In this helpful setting he wrote his *Introduction To Mathematical Philosophy*, the only snag being that when he sent the manuscript out for publication, it had to be read by an assistant governor responsible for censorship, who certainly did not find it easy going.

During the Second World War Brixton was used to detain (under regulation 18B and the Defence of the Realm Act) people suspected of sympathy with the enemy. Sir Oswald Mosley was held there until permitted to join his wife in Holloway. A single cell within the prison was placed briefly under military authority by special order of the War Minister when it held Josef Jakobs, a German officer who had landed as a spy and faced court martial (*see* Wandsworth and The Tower).

The Site Now

For a prison which was to have been demolished in 1853, Brixton has enjoyed remarkable longevity: a Georgian prison almost 170 years old, it is still the principal remand prison for an area bounded by St Albans in the north, Southend in the east, and Guildford in the south. It stands about a mile up the hill from Brixton itself, a hundred yards up a narrow cul-de-sac and screened from the main road by tenement blocks. Built before the age of grandiose gatehouses, the entrance is a plain gate in the outer wall, and anyone looking for a landmark on a first visit would do better to scan the horizon for the windmill a couple of hundred yards from the gate, which was built just three years before the prison when the entire area was farming land.

FULHAM WOMEN'S PRISON

In 1853 Fulham was still a small village outside the advancing London suburbs. It had a famous pottery, and a reputable boys' school called Burlington House. When the school moved, the Government bought the land on which it stood, and built a reformatory for young females on what had been the boys' cricket pitch.

This was the Fulham Refuge, which taught women close to the end of their prison sentences the skills which would fit them for employment as servants. Trained and ready to rejoin society, the prisoners would then be released to the home run by the Discharged Prisoners' Aid Society while waiting for a respectable post. The whole scheme was an early example of what would now be known as throughcare, based on considered forward planning from sentence to release. Prisoners gained a place in the programme not so much by their past lives or offences but 'from showing by their conduct, whilst in the previous stages at Millbank and Brixton that they are inclined to profit by the instruction provided'.

The project was a favourite of Sir Joshua Jebb, Director of Convict Prisons – the salvation of fallen women seemed to seize the imaginations of so many prominent Victorian men – and the inmates of Fulham became known as 'Jebb's pets'. The early arrivals were women who were finishing substantial sentences of four or five years, but with only 180 places Fulham could not take more than a small proportion of the 1,200 and more women behind bars in Brixton.

Fulham was intended to be distinct from other establishments, a 'place of refuge for female convicts on discharge, and not the last stage of imprisonment', but this was something of a fiction since the women were still serving their sentences in a government institution with cells and a compulsory regime. Within ten years the character of the refuge had become more rigid and severe, and a serious disturbance in 1864 caused a shift in official policy. The regime was to be that of a prison, and inmates were to eat separately in their cells for example. The refuge's original role was now being taken by charitable foundations in London and Winchester, and when a further private refuge opened seven years later in Streatham, Fulham was expanded and its title changed formally to Fulham Prison.

The prison provided accommodation for 400 women, in blocks forming three sides of a broad quadrangle, the fourth taken by an imposing chapel. The blocks had rooms for classes, work and eating on their ground floors, and the two upper storeys were divided into sleeping cells by partitions of corrugated iron – then very much a modern material, though to a modern eye it might have looked like an indoor shanty town.

Fulham Prison's capacity was larger than needed. Women now tended to receive shorter sentences, and could earn remission of one third of their terms (though men could earn only one quarter).

The Site Now

In 1888 the prison was closed, and the site sold for housing development. The shape of the original site has been totally obscured by roads and houses, but a single building remains: it had been the prison laundry, and was later used as a bottling plant for a wine shipper, before being converted in the 1980s into lavish apartments with studios. In 1985 one was placed on the market, and the estate agent's advertisement would have astounded the Victorians both by the asking price – £310,000 – and the fact that the building had been part of a prison was now being used as a selling point.

There is one final irony. That flat was sold to a member of the Royal Family, and among all the examples of royal and noble residences which became prisons – the Tower, Bridewell, the Savoy, etc. – this is the only instance I have found of a prison becoming a royal residence.

PENTONVILLE

Pentonville was built to an American pattern, to fit convicts for a life in Australia, an exotic beginning for what is now London's main prison for petty offenders.

When it opened in 1842 Pentonville was known as the Model Prison, which from the grandeur of its gatehouse to the smallest daily routine would make the clearest statement of purpose. It was regarded as successful and copied widely throughout the country, and to this day the picture retained of the British prison in most of our minds is of the imposing, galleried Pentonville.

So familiar is the image that to understand the novelty and importance of Pentonville we must recall the other London prisons of the time. The ancient prisons of the Fleet, the Marshalsea and the dourly rebuilt Newgate were ever more squalid, while Millbank was considered a costly, damp disaster. The more recent prisons at Coldbath Fields, Tothill Fields and Brixton were adequate, but reflected old concepts, and were neither impressive enough nor efficient enough for the taste of the times.

The change in thinking is still clear to a modern eye. Brixton stands back from the world down a narrow cul-de-sac, its entrance no more than a gap in the outer wall. Pentonville, with its grand frontage on an important route, and its long ramp leading to a massive gatehouse, still dominates the Caledonian Road as it did 150 years ago.

This imposing gatehouse with its false portcullis was the public face of Pentonville as the Model Prison, a new ideal.

The generation which dressed water pumping stations as castles and baronial halls looked at the fake portcullis at the entrance to the new prison and found it good. It also approved wholeheartedly of its purpose, for this was a prison which would not merely contain convicts but improve them. The second national penitentiary would make up for the disappointment of the first at Millbank and vindicate the reformers: this was to be 'the Model Prison, on the separate system' in which lessons would be learned which could be applied across the land.

Pentonville's role was to be as a processing station for prisoners about to be transported. A selection would be made at Millbank of those likely to benefit from the regime, and take the opportunity to change their ways. Sir James Graham, Home Secretary in 1841, wrote:

> I propose, therefore, that no prisoner shall be admitted into Pentonville without the knowledge that it is the portal to the penal colony, and without the certainty that he bids adieu to his connections in England, and that he must henceforth look forward to a life of labour in another hemisphere.
>
> But from the day of his entrance into the prison, while I extinguish the hope of return to his family and friends, I would open to him, fully and distinctly, the fate which awaits him, and the degree of influence which his own conduct will infallibly have over his future fortunes.

What prisoners faced was a probationary period during which they might hope to earn a ticket-of-leave which would allow great freedom to live, work, even make their fortune, in Australia; less good performers had greater restrictions imposed on them, and could keep only part of their pay, while the worst would spend their period of transportation in a labour gang without pay.

The 'portal to the penal colony' was the gatehouse, which was important not only for its design but for its designer, Sir Charles Barry. As architect of the new Houses of Parliament, Barry was both fashionable and a representative of the highest Establishment taste; that he should be offered – and accept – a commission for a prison entrance was a measure of the importance of Pentonville.

Beyond the gate is a central block with an 'Italian' clocktower, and from here radiate four utilitarian wings. The radial plan was borrowed from a much-admired penitentiary in Philadelphia because it offered a solution to several design problems. If prisoners were to be held in individual cells, how could they best be observed and controlled? The Millbank solution, of ringing a central vantage point with cells, was unnecessarily complex and costly to build, and inefficient compared with stacking galleried landings on either side of a central straight corridor. If more than one such straight block were required, it seemed sensible to have them all meet at a central point to allow a minimal staff to keep an eye on all wings at once. A cross shape was part of an answer, and used elsewhere, but the fan-shaped radial plan allowed more blocks to be set within a limited area, and seemed so apt a design that within ten years of the opening of Pentonville more than fifty prisons were built in Britain on the same pattern, most of which survive today. The shape was not perfect, causing difficulties with light and ventilation, but it served well enough the aims of the time.

The prison regime followed faithfully the principle of separation. Prisoners wore masks to prevent communication or recognition, and worked, ate and slept alone in their cells. In the early part of his sentence a prisoner took exercise in a small yard on his own, supervised by unseen guards in small observation posts. Later, he would be allowed to walk around a larger yard at the same time as other prisoners, though forbidden to communicate. Convicts taking such exercise, or moving about the prison, had a most sinister appearance: each was required to wear a mask, a cap pulled so low that the prisoner looked out through two holes cut for his eyes above the peak. Mayhew found

> . . . the costume of the men seems like the outward vestment to some wandering soul rather than that of a human being; for the eyes, glistening through the apertures in the mask, give one the notion of a spirit peeping out behind it, so that there is something positively terrible in the idea that these are men whose crimes have caused their very features to be hidden from the world.

This exacting regime was intended for the more robust convicts, those best fitted to learn and benefit before their transportation, but evidence was growing that prolonged solitary confinement was sending prisoners mad, and driving others to suicide. As transportation was replaced by long terms with hard labour at home, Pentonville became part of the new convict system, selection ended, and any and all convicts might be sent there, including boys. There were still some determined reformers who wanted the regime to continue unchanged, but even the chaplain of Pentonville was forced to concede that 'Separate confinement is no panacea for criminal depravity. It has been supposed capable of reforming a man from habits of theft to a life of honesty, from vice to virtue. It has no such power. No human punishment has ever done this.'

Changes were made. The small exercise yards were replaced by a single large space, the partitions which separated convicts even in prayer in the chapel were removed, and the masks were abolished. Pentonville was still to be a short-term depot for prisoners on their way to other establishments, but the period to be served there was cut from one year to nine months.

Pentonville retained this role as an initial clearing-house until 1877, when as part of the larger changes following centralization of prison control it became a local prison, receiving shorter-term prisoners from the London area.

After the closure of Newgate in 1902 the gallows used there was removed to Pentonville, which then served north London as a hanging prison (its counterpart in the south was Wandsworth). Sir Roger Casement, the Irish patriot convicted in 1916 of soliciting German help in the rebel cause, Dr Crippen and the poisoner Seddon were among those executed at the prison.

The Site Now

There were proposals to close Pentonville in 1939, but it continues as the principal local prison for the London area. Little changed in more than 140 years, the prison still looms in Caledonian Road about a mile north of King's Cross station.

SEPARATION AND SILENCE

There is a very old saying that we must always be careful in making our wishes, in case they come true. It was the dream of the prison reformers of the late eighteenth century that prisons should not just confine, but reform their inmates. They visited, and protested about, prisons which were crowded, disorderly, bawdy, and prisons in which the weak and poor were the prey of the strong, and the innocent were led astray.

A case could be made, both practical and humane, for holding prisoners in well-ordered separation, to preserve them from the contagions of disease, criminality and exploitation, and allow them to serve their sentences with dignity. It was even advanced as an argument for providing free and nourishing food that it was better to pay for the food than allow separation to be interrupted by visits from friends and relatives bearing meals.

John Howard set out the advantages: 'I wish to have so many small rooms or cabins that each criminal may sleep alone . . . The separation I am pleading for, especially at night, would prevent escapes or make them very difficult . . . This would also prevent their robbing another in the night.' He was opposed to full-time solitary confinement, but touched on the idea which was to seize the imaginations of so many others: 'Solitude and silence are favourable to reflection; and may possibly lead to repentance.'

There was something in the idea of enforced solitude which appealed to religious men of a certain gloomy, hell-fire disposition, who believed that if only all other communication and distraction could be removed, and a criminal receive thorough preaching and the opportunity to read instructional and inspirational texts, he would come to repentance and reformation. 'Dejection and solitude are the natural parents of reflection', and hard physical toil would help the process, if it were of the kind prescribed in the National Penitentiary Act of 1778: 'Labour of the hardest and most servile Kind, in which Drudgery is chiefly required . . .'

Of course, attempts to impose such a regime achieved nothing, but the answer of the believers was rather like that of apologists for other vastly brutal schemes like Soviet farm collectivization – the idea was sound, betrayed only by those too soft-hearted to take it to its proper conclusion.

An alternative which found its own supporters was the silent associated system in which men went about their work and exercise together, but were not permitted to communicate. Battle was joined between the advocates of each system, and in the middle of the nineteenth century it looked as if the separators would prevail. Prisons were designed with their system in mind, so that to this day some prisons simply do not have any sizeable rooms other than the chapel in which numbers of men can congregate. But evidence was accumulating of the ill effects on mental health of strict solitary confinement, and it was limited to ever-shorter periods at the very start of sentences, to be followed by silent association with other convicts in which it was acknowledged that covert communication was unavoidable.

By the end of the century there was great pressure from outside the prison system to permit associated work and removal of the Rule of Silence. There were practical difficulties in providing workplaces in which men might work together under supervision, and only grudgingly was any conversation permitted: 'The privilege of talking may be given after a certain period as a reward for good conduct.' Not until 1922 was the rule substantially modified. Acceptance of these changes was much quicker once prison staff realized that the disciplinary effect of withdrawing, or threatening to withdraw, the privilege of mixing and talking with fellow-prisoners helped them to run their prisons more smoothly.

This protracted contest of ideas affected not only the day-to-day life of prisoners, but the very shape and construction of the prisons in which they were held.

Elizabeth Fry was not a sentimental woman, nor an alarmist, but in the separatist gaols she saw the dungeons of the future, and of the life within them said: 'I do not believe that a despairing or stupefied state is suitable for salvation.'

WANDSWORTH

Since the middle of the last century the west side of Wandsworth Common has been dominated by a vast prison. The description published by Henry Mayhew after his visit in 1856 is splendidly damning:

The House of Correction at Wandsworth has, externally, little to recommend it to the eye, having none of the fine, gloomy character and solemnity of Newgate, nor any of the castellated grandeur of the City Prison at Holloway; neither can it be said to partake of the massive simplicity of the exterior of Tothill Fields, nor to possess any feature about it that will bear comparison with the noble portcullis gateway at Pentonville.

To speak plainly, the exterior of the Surrey House of Correction is mean and ill-proportioned to the last degree, while the architecture of the outbuildings exhibits all the bad taste of Cockney-Italian villas, and none of the austere impressiveness that should belong to a building of penal character. Again, the central mass rising behind the stunted gateway is heavy even to clumsiness, and the whole aspect of the structure uncommanding as a Methodist college.

Reading this diatribe it is hard not to feel some sympathy for architect D. R. Hill of Birmingham, to whose design the prison had been completed only four years before Mayhew's visit. The commission was to design a gaol which would replace the other Surrey houses of correction at Brixton, Kingston and Guildford, which were overcrowded. The Surrey Justices wanted to be able to accommodate 750 prisoners immediately, and to be able to expand the new prison as and when necessary. The site had to be within a mile of a railway station, so as not to expend on travel costs the savings realized by using cheaper land far out of town.

Wandsworth was built to the conventional radial design within an enormous twenty-six-acre site, which includes streets and fields well outside the walls. Radial plans were used for two separate blocks, with male prisoners in a five-, later six-wing block, and females in a smaller two-wing block to which a third wing was added when demand rose. At the time of Mayhew's visit, each wing had three storeys or landings, but this was later increased to four. The separate system was used at first, and the cells were nearly as large as the exemplary ones at Pentonville, each having a water closet, a gas light, and a hammock.

To maintain separation, prisoners' faces were hidden, the men by a type of hood, the women by a veil. The prisoner's register number was painted on each simple uniform; and a brass tally on the left arm of a man, or on the belt of a woman, carried the location of the individual's cell as a combination of wing letter, landing and cell numbers. This same location code was shown on the small stall which the prisoner would occupy in chapel, and during the day any warder speaking to a prisoner would address him or her by the cell number.

Wandsworth was a local prison for those serving short sentences, a House of Correction, and the regime included the hard work now traditional in such places. A very few were employed in skilled work, but many wasted their energies on Wandsworth's alternative to the treadwheel, the handcranked hard-labour machine. Handcranks also pumped water from the prison's well, and ground flour for use in the kitchens. The most common work for men was the inevitable oakum-picking, while the 166 female prisoners were mainly employed in the laundry.

When prisons were nationalized in 1877 Wandsworth was absorbed into the new system as a short-term prison. It had been regarded as one of the better gaols, constructed and operated in keeping with current ideas of good practice. There was a more sinister change of use from 1878 when Wandsworth took over from Horsemonger Lane as the hanging prison for south London.

As the national prison system developed, Wandsworth came to be used for recidivists and after the First World War the smaller block was taken over as the 'Boys' Prison' for London, under a separate governor and regime from the main block. This was a place in which youths were assessed so that reports could be sent to courts and, if they were sentenced to Borstal training, to allocate them.

In 1929 this role was given to Wormwood Scrubs, not least because it was felt that young people who were not yet hardened criminals should not be held in a hanging gaol. On the other hand, it was seen as fitting to use Wandsworth for Borstal absconders and others needing a more 'corrective' regime.

Within two days of the declaration of war in 1939, Wandsworth received one of its oddest prisoners. A Welshman called Owens had been recruited by the *Abwehr*, German military intelligence, but was also on the books of MI5. His true loyalties were never clear, but he presented himself to the police on 4 September 1939 and offered his radio transmitter and instructions, and said that he would be willing to transmit to Germany. From his cell in Wandsworth he tapped out: MUST MEET YOU IN HOLLAND AT ONCE. BRING WEATHER CODE. RADIO TOWN AND HOTEL WALES READY. He was requesting a meeting, asking for codes which would enable him to send meteorological information, and claiming to have recruited Welsh nationalist saboteurs. In Hamburg this was accepted as a genuine message, and the Double Cross System (*see* Latchmere House) was born.

Across the main road from Wandsworth Prison was the Royal Victoria Patriotic School, used as a clearing station for refugees arriving from occupied Europe. Among them were spies and several were tried swiftly and secretly before delivery to Wandsworth for execution. The last person to be executed at The Tower was held here; the Wandsworth governor of the time was impressed by the calm dignity of the spy Josef Jakobs as he left under military escort on his final morning in 1941. The hangings continued after the war. William Joyce, whose trial still provokes legal debate, but who was reviled by the British public as the 'Lord Haw Haw' who had broadcast defeatism to them from Berlin, was executed at Wandsworth in January 1946. To this day the prison retains the only gallows in the British prison system.

In recent years Wandsworth has been used as the prison in which men who have been convicted but not sentenced are held, and as a depot for convicted men who are to be allocated or re-allocated to other prisons; most recently the smaller block of wings has become a centre for prisoners held under Rule 43 – that is, men kept apart from the main population because their offences or behaviour put them at risk of victimization: usually sex offenders.

The Site Now

Wandsworth Prison stands a hundred yards to the west of Trinity Road, about three-quarters of a mile south of Wandsworth Bridge. A short avenue of trees leads to the gatehouse, but the view has been much spoiled by a curtain wall built some years ago to shield the gate itself.

HOLLOWAY

Holloway is Britain's principal prison for women, and the only prison in Inner London to have been built this century. The story of Holloway is of two prisons on the same site: a City overspill gaol which became a national women's prison in 1902, and a modern prison completed only in 1983.

The Old Holloway

In the 1840s the Corporation of the City of London proposed to build a house of correction, a local prison for those serving shorter sentences. A report was prepared which dismissed a variety of sites in the City as too expensive and impractical – the land there was costly, and an extension of Giltspur Street, Newgate or Whitecross

Street would not offer sufficient extra accommodation.

To move out of the City would save at least £130,000, as well as offering greater space in healthier surroundings. Most conveniently, the City owned a tract of land which would serve very well, the ten acres it had bought in Holloway to be used as a cemetery during an outbreak of cholera. The site was three times the size of any alternative, clear of buildings and well-drained.

The prison was designed by J. B. Bunning and had six wings – four large wings for men, and a smaller wing each for women and juveniles. The capacity was for 438 prisoners, and the total cost was only £92,700. The statistics conceal the most remarkable feature of Holloway – its appearance.

Even now there are prisons within ancient castles – Oxford (first built in 1071) and Lancaster (1094), and of course the Tower. What the City commissioned at Holloway was a brand-new prison that tried hard to look like a medieval fortress. The central tower was intended as a copy of Caesar's Tower at Warwick Castle, and rose above 'a noble building of castellated Gothic'. (There are those who still brood about the brutal demolition of the Euston Arch, and many like the author who are still cross about the shifty destruction of Holloway's gatehouse.) Only three fragments survive from the decorative detail of the old prison: a pair of griffins which guarded the inner gate now look rather forlorn flanking a walkway within the new campus, and the original glass foundation stone, bearing the words 'MAY GOD PRESERVE THE CITY OF LONDON AND MAKE THIS PLACE A TERROR TO EVIL DOERS', which has been preserved as a curiosity.

All this flamboyance was not only intended as an expression of civic pride and penal intent, but also to reassure neighbours in a rising middle-class suburb.

Holloway was the largest of the City's prisons. As a house of correction its regime was not as severe as that in Pentonville, its close contemporary. Although silence was enforced, and all other communication forbidden, the prisoners worked and took classes together. Productive work of many kinds, from basketmaking to gardening, was provided, and the treadwheel was put to use in raising water from a well below the prison. The practical nature of the regime extended to compulsory classes for those serving more than six months. Reading and writing, arithmetic, geography and history were all taught in classes, and individual tuition was available in prisoners' own cells. Well-educated prisoners were excused the classes, but were obliged to spend the session writing a precis of the sermon at that morning's service – chapel attendance was daily, and compulsory.

Extraordinary to the modern observer is the size of the staff – the prison was run by no more than thirty-two people, from governor to messenger. Of these, no more than twenty were uniformed discipline staff (officers who control and supervise), clear evidence that in prison the control is by consent of the mass of inmates. For all this, there were irrational fears in government circles about prison security and discipline, and following Home Office recommendations in 1867 Holloway was provided with seventeen pistols, twenty-four rifles and seventeen cutlasses – a considerable burden for the available officers, and likely to send them into the fray looking like comic pirates. The true risks were small: it was not until the 1950s that any prisoner escaped from within Holloway.

Staff efficiency was promoted both by the prison's high standards and by a set of penalties which included fines for failure to lock a cell (one shilling), 'wrangling on duty' (one shilling), falling asleep in chapel (sixpence – perhaps a more common offence), and failing to provide a prisoner with writing paper (also sixpence). Officers were firmly instructed to conduct themselves calmly. Though rigorous in its expectations, the City was a loyal employer: when the prison was nationalized and the staff taken on to the government payroll, the City gave gratuities to the officers, and continued for the next forty years to administer a pension scheme for them.

Shortly before nationalization of prisons in 1870, Holloway received its first debtors, transferred from Whitecross Street when it closed down.

After its absorption into the state system in 1877, Holloway became more crowded, and a large proportion of the prisoners were subject to the rigours of Second Division imprisonment which carried few comforts or privileges. For those in the First Division, Holloway life could be quite bearable, as the account by W. T. Stead reveals.

Stead was not the only notable to be held in Holloway. Oscar Wilde was first imprisoned there, awaiting bail for five weeks in 1895. Less than a year later Holloway featured in an international incident when it received Dr Jameson, who had led a raid into Boer territory. Captured in an ambush he was freed by Kruger on condition that he returned to England to stand trial under the Foreign Enlistment Act, and served eighteen months in Holloway. On his release he returned to South Africa, and became Premier of the Cape Colony in 1904.

Wilde and Jameson served their sentences during the brief period from 1892 to 1902 when Holloway held only male prisoners. All female prisoners in the London area were taken to Woking in 1892, in one of the sudden policy changes familiar to anyone who has worked in the national prison system. Just ten years later there was a complete reversal, and since then Holloway has almost exclusively held female prisoners.

In 1906 the first suffragettes were committed to Holloway, beginning a period of conflict and public concern which lasted until the First World War. The prison was the focus of great public attention as the struggle for votes for women which was being fought in the street took new forms behind the imposing walls of the gaol.

Several factors combined to create this interest. Firstly, prisons were now hidden places, no longer open to casual visitors, and had become more sinister in the public eye. And whereas in the past women in prison had usually been petty thieves and prostitutes, objects of pity but without a voice, the suffragettes had changed all that. Articulate, confident and determined, many with formidable education and social standing, they were eager to bring their experiences of prison to the public's attention. They deliberately chose to go to prison as an alternative to paying fines, and their numbers grew as it became one of the campaign's objectives to fill the prisons to overflowing, with seventy-five women being taken into Holloway on a single day in 1907.

Public interest turned into indignation when the authorities mishandled the suffragettes' hunger strikes. In 1909 Marion Wallace-Dunlop was released after just four days of hunger strike, shunning attempts by the staff to tempt her with what was probably the best food ever offered to a prisoner. More prisoners gained their freedom this way, to the frustration of the Government, which ordered forcible feeding. The procedure of pumping liquids through a rubber tube inserted through the nose or mouth, was condemned by the Press and public – more than 100 eminent doctors petitioned the Home Secretary. The death of King Edward VII and a change of government brought a lull, but in March 1912 Holloway received more than 200 new prisoners after a window-breaking progress down Oxford Street, and the hunger strikes began again. This time the official response was the 1913 Prisoners (Temporary Discharge) Act – the 'Cat and Mouse Act', by which prisoners could be released if showing ill-health through hunger strike, yet rearrested if they broke certain regulations.

Mary Richardson was a Holloway hunger striker who was offered release if she would cease her activities. She refused, saying: 'They cannot do more than kill me.' The doctor's reply was: 'Unfortunately, it is not a question of killing you. You will be kept here until you are a skeleton and a nervous and mental wreck, and then you will be sent to an institution where they look after mental wrecks.'

Newspapers were now able to use photographs, and press photographers recording the arrivals and departures made the entrances of Holloway familiar to the whole country. Their colleagues prepared features on the life, regime, uniform and conditions behind the famous gates.

The First World War brought an effective end to the suffragette campaign and before the Armistice the first women gained the vote. In 1922 public attention was again focused on the prison with the arrest and trial of Edith Thompson, accused with her lover of the murder of her husband. It is clear now that Mrs Thompson had no part in the planning or the killing, but was convicted and condemned for her adultery. In January 1923 she and her lover were hanged simultaneously, he at Pentonville, she at Holloway in the prison's first execution. Popular feeling ran high in her favour, and there were many ready to believe the most grisly stories of the hanging. Thirty years later it emerged that she had in fact been quite heavily sedated and carried to the scaffold. The truth was less dramatic than the rumour, but was powerfully poignant, and the Thompson case was repeatedly raised in the debates on capital punishment.

Between the wars attempts were made to improve the prison's conditions. A hostel was opened nearby for discharged prisoners, an earnings scheme helped to provide a small nest-egg on release, physical conditions were improved, and a charitable interest was shown by many bodies and organizations. By the 1930s it had become plain that the building itself was the main restriction on further improvement and in 1938 Sir Samuel Hoare, a great-nephew of Elizabeth Fry, introduced a bill for a major rebuilding programme.

The Second World War put an end to such planning. Holloway was emptied within days of the outbreak of war, with short-term prisoners discharged and long-termers transferred to Aylesbury Prison in Buckinghamshire. Holloway was to take people detained under Regulation 18B – those whose actions might be 'prejudicial to the conduct of the war'. Anyone who might join a Fifth Column, such as members of the British Union of Fascists or other groups sympathetic to Nazism, was to be swept in, and among these potential traitors sent to Holloway was Lady Mosley, who was joined there by Sir Oswald, from Brixton. But among the detainees were many who had been arrested solely because of being aliens, and by an irony there were also those who had come to Britain as refugees from Nazi oppression. Most of the detainees had been released by early 1941, and by 1942, as the danger of invasion or blitz faded, Holloway received back most of its prisoners.

Also in 1942 the Prison Commissioners prepared a report which proposed the spreading of women prisoners among several smaller prisons around the country. Nothing came of this, but in 1945 Holloway gained its first woman governor, Dr Charity Taylor.

There were to be two more executions at Holloway, one rarely remembered and one lastingly notorious. Two women were hanged, within ten months of each other, for murders committed two hundred yards apart in the same Hampstead street. The world remembers Ruth Ellis, the last woman to be executed in Britain, from articles, books and a film which have told how she was betrayed by her lover, shot him in a Hampstead street, and then seemed determined to die. But the year before Ellis's execution a Mrs Christofi had gone to the scaffold without such public sympathy; she had jealously killed her son's wife, battering her to death and trying to burn the body. At her trial it came out that this unstable woman had tried some years before to kill her own mother-in-law in Cyprus, and there can be little doubt that if tried today she would be sent to Broadmoor, not to the gallows.

The New Holloway

In 1968 the Home Secretary James Callaghan announced a programme 'to reshape the system of female penal establishments in England and Wales'. The advantages of keeping a single women's prison in London where it was accessible to courts and visitors had prevailed over the idea of scattering its population. The prison was not to be closed, but rebuilt steadily on the same site while continuing to function.

There were high hopes of the new Holloway, which both in its design and its regime marked a radical change from its predecessors. It was designed with a campus built around a central 'village green' – one of the Project Group which planned the changes said she would rather 'imprison women in a park than park them in a prison'. In its outline and its detail the design would conceal the evidence of containment – the buildings themselves would screen the sinuous perimeter wall from view, while the windows would carry no old-fashioned bars, but be made up of tall narrow panels, to the same effect.

The wings would resemble modern students' halls of residence, most prisoners sharing large airy rooms, in a grand departure from single-cell blocks, and clustered around would be units in which communal activities and therapeutic services would be close at hand.

The central concept was closer to that of a hospital than a prison, with medical, obstetric and psychological units offering support and therapy, which would remain available to prisoners on an out-patient scheme even after release. It had been suggested in the planning stages that this was an establishment which could be turned over to the National Health Service for use as a mental hospital if penal plans ever changed.

The Site Now

Demolition of the old Holloway began in 1971, and the slow process of replacement took twelve years to complete. The new prison has none of the contrived stateliness of the old, and stands on the north side of Parkhurst Road a few hundred yards west of the junction with Holloway Road. The original gateway stood squarely opposite the end of Caledonian Road, a little up the hill from the more discreet modern entrance.

W. T. STEAD

In 1885 W. T. Stead, the editor of the *Pall Mall Gazette*, was imprisoned for two months in Holloway. His crime was that in campaigning to draw attention to child prostitution he had bought a girl from her mother, and reported the transaction in articles headed 'The Maiden Tribute of Modern Babylon'. The mother denied selling her daughter for immoral purposes, and Stead was eventually tried. Sent first to Coldbath Fields, Stead was

suddenly whisked to Holloway and granted more
than customary privileges, in recognition that he had
no criminal intent, but also perhaps to make sure that
his influential magazine did not attack the prison
system. If that was the aim, it was achieved. Stead's
account of Holloway was downright enthusiastic.

> I had papers, books, letters, flowers, everything
> that heart could wish. I had my own little kettle,
> and made my own tea; fresh eggs were sent
> by some unknown benefactor in Ireland, and
> everything in the shape of food was ordered
> from outside. I was allowed my own hearth-
> rug, and easy chairs as well as writing desk and
> cosy little tea-table. I could take exercise when
> I pleased for as long as I pleased in daytime. I
> worked at my own trade throughout my term.
> I got the newspapers every morning at 7.15 and
> at 10.00 the messenger got his copy. From the
> Governor, Colonel Millman, to the poor fellow
> who scrubbed out my room, everyone was as
> kind as could be. Twice a week my wife brought
> the sunlight of her presence into the pretty little
> room, all hung round with Christmas greetings
> from absent friends. On the day after Christmas
> the whole family came, and what high jinks we
> had in the old gaol with all the bairns! The room
> was rather small for blind man's buff, but we
> managed it somehow, and never was there a
> merrier little party than that which met in cell
> number two on the ground floor of the East Wing
> of Holloway Gaol.

WORMWOOD SCRUBS

Wormwood Scrubs was built due to Millbank Penitentiary being an expensive flop. That first national penitentiary had been the result of armchair theorizing about design and regime, where practicality had been sacrificed to the pursuit of ideals in everything from the choice of site to the layout of the corridors.

This was the view of the Directors of Convict Prisons in the 1870s, and with Victorian resolve and an eye to the future they cast about for a new site which would be set apart from central London, but accessible by road and rail. In East Acton they found about twenty acres of heavy clay, suitable for making bricks; it belonged to the Ecclesiastical Commissioners, and formed a part of the open grassland called Wormwood Scrubs.

The site was bought in 1873, and thorough plans drawn up for using convict labour, on the site and in the workshops of other prisons, to assemble the prison. In this way the prisoners would learn trades, the Commissioners would retain an overall control impossible if the work were contracted out, and above all the prison would be cheaper.

The design was conceived by the chairman of the directors himself, Major-General Edmund Du Cane – the road on which the prison stands carries his name. He rejected not only the complexity of the Millbank fiasco, but even the radial shape which had become conventional. 'The idea of making blocks radiate from a common centre was abandoned . . .', he wrote. 'The cell blocks, therefore, are arranged in parallel, running north to south . . . All the cells under this arrangement can have some light on them at some time of day. There are no damp, dark corners or courts as there must necessarily be in a radiating plan and the cell windows of one block do not overlook the yard attached to another block.'

The four blocks were to be connected by covered passageways, with the kitchen, bakehouse and boilerhouse placed between the central pair, and other buildings assembled about this core. Particular importance was attached to the gatehouse: '. . . the most important addition to the prison, not only as being a sufficiently strong entrance to the establishment but also that it contains accommodation for and is occupied by all the single discipline officers of the prison who would be available for immediate service at night should an emergency arise.' There must have been a good practical case for a large, strong gate, but even in this most businesslike of schemes Du Cane was tempted to use the gatehouse as a symbol, as a way of impressing upon the public his intentions. Du Cane wasn't going to conjure up the grimness of Newgate or the Gothic romanticism of Holloway: his gate had all the strength and mob resistance needed, but carries portraits of two reformers – Howard and Fry – high on either side.

The design having been decided upon, the complex work of construction began from a few iron-lined wooden huts. Because Du Cane thought the public might be alarmed by daily movements of convicts through the streets he had the huts prefabricated at Millbank and Pentonville, then installed ready for the first one hundred men to live on site. Around this temporary shelter the convicts built themselves a prison, occupying each block as it rose. Even part-completed blocks were roofed with tarpaulin so that the lower floors could be occupied in turn.

Access roads had to be laid, with materials drawn across the open fields on sledges. The on-site clay provided 35,000,000 bricks; from Dartmoor and Portland came stone, Portland also sending iron castings. Carpenters, joiners and blacksmiths from Millbank and Chatham were also put to use. It was an enormous enterprise, but was carried out well. Two prisoners died in an accidental fall, but an outbreak of typhoid was contained without loss of life. Only one prisoner escaped of the 7,030 who passed through during the prison's construction, since around the encampment were huts for a civil guard of ex-soldiers armed with rifles.

The finished prison made a good impression on visitors. To Victorians used to the grimness of Newgate, and with an appetite for the decorative, Wormwood Scrubs was a marvel. The Scrubs was built after the St Pancras Hotel and Leeds Town Hall, just before the Victoria and Albert and other great museums of South Kensington. An early visitor was delighted that: 'On all hands are flower beds, brilliant with multi-coloured blossoms; on your right is a beautiful marble colonnade, round the pillars of which gay creepers intertwine; on your left are arbours of luscious greenery . . . All is bright with the joyous garb of the affluent life, and bathed in the warmth of golden sunlight.' It is easy to cavil that the colonnade was in fact Portland stone, that the weather has not always been so fine in East Acton, and that much of that garden has been lost to demands for space and better security, but it is true that a wholehearted attempt had been made to give the prison a new and more pleasant atmosphere.

There was another response from visitors which we may find less attractive.

The prisoners have evidently most healthy quarters at Wormwood Scrubs and have much to be thankful for, but they are not thankful. They reck not of the old prison days, of dark cells, unwholesome air, and gaol fever, they are not grateful that the philanthropists and prison boards and Royal Commission have studied them and made much of them during the last quarter century. They are not a grateful class . . .

Perhaps they just couldn't find words to express to the Home Secretary their gratitude that being locked up for years for petty theft no longer carried a high risk of death from typhoid.

Wormwood Scrubs was to have been a national long-term penitentiary, but in the year that the last of the cell blocks was completed and filled, the entire purpose of the prison was changed. It would now be a local gaol taking short-term petty offenders. Local Londoners worried about this, because they feared that, whereas the original inmates were to have been transferred to Portland, Chatham and Dartmoor before their release, the new prisoners would spill out of the gates into the neighbourhood and their visitors bring trouble. A petition was circulated and public meetings called. A promise was given that the Scrubs would hold only those serving more than three months. The promise wasn't kept, but it didn't matter, since none of the gloomy predictions came true.

As the prison's use changed, the first women prisoners arrived, to be held, as elsewhere, in cells built slightly small for them. Just eleven years later, they were moved to Holloway, and in their place came the debtors, still a stock-in-trade of local gaols. During the early years of the twentieth-century debtors were both better and worse off than their predecessors in the City compters. Prison life was healthier, but debtors were now obliged to work like other prisoners and could no longer choose and buy their own food. And although they were privileged with extra exercise time, visits and letters, their status was now very little different from that of criminals. They might keep their own clothes rather than take prison uniform, but many of them were so poorly dressed on arrival that they were only too pleased to put on the drab clothes of the convict.

Life in the prison was hard. Du Cane was a reformer,

but he was an austere man who held to ideas popular early in the nineteenth century. Separation had a strong appeal to him, and he applied great pressure to substitute individual tuition for classes; labour was central to his view, and the cranks and treadmills turned at Wormwood Scrubs, though they were later used only for those men sentenced to hard labour.

Du Cane retired in 1895, and in that year the Gladstone Committee put forward proposals for reform. Among the Committee's concerns was more appropriate treatment of young offenders, and from this grew the Borstal system. This was a new kind of institution, named after the village in Kent where the first was established. The basic principles were the separation of youths from older, corrupting criminals, training in useful skills, and an encouragement to work in teams which followed a public school rather than a prison pattern.

Where no separate institution was available, young prisoners would be put in local prisons under the 'modified Borstal system'. Wormwood Scrubs operated such a scheme from 1904. A range of trades was taught, and literacy taught from 1907 in a new lecture hall. Each week a guest lecturer was invited to address the youths on a useful or moral theme. Borstal was at first an internal prison change for young men whose sentence had been imprisonment, but from 1908 courts could impose Borstal training, in which the term was not fixed. The maximum time servable was three years, but a young man could earn his release on licence after six months, and a young woman after three months. (This system remained in operation until 1983, when the Borstal system was replaced by a youth custody scheme in which sentences were of fixed length though the maximum time was reduced to two years.)

As the system developed, each new Borstal took on a

different role and character, and at Wormwood Scrubs a block was set aside as an allocation centre in which freshly-sentenced trainees could be assessed before being sent to the Borstal most suited to them.

Changes were being made in the adult wings, too. To meet the old concern that old lags contaminated newcomers, first-time prisoners were classified as 'star' prisoners, and Wormwood Scrubs came to specialize in holding them. The Stage System was introduced, and the Scrubs settled into a couple of decades of relatively calm progress.

Ten days before the outbreak of the Second World War the Borstal trainees were moved out to Feltham. Part of the prison was evacuated, and with an attempt at stealth the War Department moved in. Secrecy was not easily maintained, and it may be true that conductors on the No 72 bus route would announce 'All change for MI5!' when stopping by the prison gate. The rapidly expanding MI5 bureaucracy moved into the prison, but not without practical difficulties. Cell doors are not designed to be opened from inside, and so were left ajar, which did nothing for the confidentiality of conversations. The Scrubs was too large, too visible and too insecure for the most delicate interrogation, and before long Latchmere House had been adapted for the work.

In 1939 Wormwood Scrubs even found a place in the history of nuclear weapons. Heavy water was a material used in controlling atomic reactions, a rare commodity which was denied to the Germans by the famous attack on the Norsk Hydro plant in Norway, as anyone who saw the film *Heroes of Telemark* will recall. The world's entire supply was brought to London by two scientists escaping from France, and was lodged in Wormwood Scrubs in twenty-six cans containing 185 kilograms, worth many times their weight in gold. From the Scrubs the containers were 'gradually transferred to a fortress at the other end of the social scale: they were put in the charge of the Librarian of Windsor Castle'.

For a time no prisoners were held at all, but, in 1942, 324 inmates were received from Wandsworth, and the regime returned steadily to normal. Although no executions have ever been carried out in Wormwood Scrubs, a part of the hospital wing was used as condemned quarters towards the end of the war, for those who would later be hanged at Pentonville and Wandsworth, including William Joyce (Lord Haw Haw).

The single post-war event which drew public attention to Wormwood Scrubs was the escape in 1966 of George Blake. He had been given the longest fixed sentence ever imposed by an English court – forty-two years – for spying, but he made his way through a window, across roofs, and finally over a wall with the help of accomplices – one, a Republican Irishman, wrote a book about the escape, and in 1987 two British anti-nuclear campaigners were identified as having taken part in the plot.

Blake's escape prompted a major review of prison security under Lord Mountbatten and much tighter restrictions were imposed on prisoners who were seen as dangerous or whose escape, like Blake's, would embarrass the Government.

Wormwood Scrubs now holds a wing in which life-sentence prisoners are assessed in the early years of their terms, and lower security accommodation for remand and short-term prisoners.

The Site Now
Protected by twentieth-century outer gates, fences and electronic security, Wormwood Scrubs Prison stands on Du Cane Road, just north of Westway in East Acton.

LATCHMERE HOUSE

In 1939 the Security Service (MI5) needed an interrogation centre through which to process suspected spies; their first administration was in Wormwood Scrubs, but they found the prison too public.

There are few places in Greater London which can be described as secluded. Latchmere House, on a quiet dead-end road off Ham Common, was chosen to receive prisoners because it offered a valuable combination of obscurity and easy access to the capital. This Victorian mansion, which had been taken over by the War Office many years before as a recuperation centre for officers shell-shocked in the First World War, met MI5's needs well, with its large grounds protected from prying eyes by a screen of trees. Behind extra fences a compound was quickly constructed, with a small cell block, exercise yards, and barrack huts for the guards.

The official name for this new centre was part of an extended pun. MI5 wanted to 'turn' agents when they were caught, in other words to have them keep in touch with their German masters, but firmly under British control, sending only information that would mislead. This was a double cross; XX in Roman numerals stands for 20; the committee running the operation was therefore known as the Twenty Committee, and Latchmere House, as the home of the operation, became Camp 020. (There was one other numbered centre: Camp 001 was the hospital wing of Dartmoor Prison, used to hold internees who had to be distanced and quarantined from other prisoners.)

Camp 020 grew quickly. The original twenty-odd cells were not enough, and in 1941 a further block of ninety-two cells was added. (In the same building programme, each of the original cells was bugged with a microphone.) Even this expanded accommodation was soon too small to

meet the demand, and a further centre was built on Lord
Nuffield's estate near Henley – still a penal establishment,
this is now Huntercombe Youth Custody Centre.

Suspects were interrogated at Latchmere House, and
the fate of those identified as spies was decided by the
'Hanging Committee'. This group of interrogators had
effective power of life and death – those whom they
chose to spare were used to feed bogus information to
Germany, but those they rejected went to secret trial,
where only one sentence was available in cases of treachery.
A single defendant was acquitted; fifteen others went to the
scaffolds at Pentonville and Wandsworth. One more, tried
by court martial because he held military rank, was shot
at the Tower; this was Josef Jakobs, who made such an
impression on the governor of Wandsworth.

Latchmere House is now a remand centre for juveniles,
very few of whom can know the establishment's sinister
history.

The Site Now
Latchmere House is to be found on Church Road, a lane
running from Ham Common towards Richmond Park.

THE BROAD ARROW

No symbol of the prisoner is as quickly recognized
as the broad arrow, still a favourite of cartoonists
even though the arrowed uniforms were abolished
in 1922, and had been worn only for about fifty years
before that.

The famous arrow was not originally associated
with prisons, but was used to identify government
property, and the device is still found on the labels
of military uniforms and equipment. It was first
adopted by Henry, Earl of Romney when he was

Master General of the Ordnance from 1693 to 1702. His personal heraldic cognizance or symbol was a pheon, or broad arrow, and was applied to the stores in his charge.

When applied to prison uniform, the arrow was useful in deterring escapers and absconders, who would have found it difficult to wander at large in such distinctive clothes. To the Victorians it seemed important to create a 'dress of shame' to emphasize the wretchedness of the offender, and the arrow motif served their purpose.

In today's prisons only convicted men are obliged to wear regulation clothes, of ordinary working blue jeans or dungarees and a T-shirt or conventional striped shirt. There is no uniform for women, and male civil prisoners may wear a brown working outfit. At the moment no uniform is issued to remanded untried men, though this may change. Prisoners who had escaped or absconded may be placed in 'patches' for a time when back in custody. In this uniform some of the panels of blue cloth are replaced with yellow to catch the eye. These yellow patches were originally sewn on to clothes, but could very easily be removed – a man resourceful enough to escape was hardly likely to be confounded by a few stitches.

OTHER PUNISHMENTS

Imprisonment and death have never been the only punishments meted out to offenders. We have become used to the idea that the natural penalty for crime is to lock up the culprit, but there were many other ways of dealing with crime, and many lasted alongside the increasing use of imprisonment.

The commonest punishment for petty offending was simple public humiliation, sometimes with discomfort, pain or risk. In the small world of early London, culprits would usually be known to the entire neighbourhood, and the stigma of public exposure would have a lasting effect. For trivial offences, a defendant might simply be obliged to stand on a high stool in a public place, while the offence was announced to the crowd. More elaborate penalties might be concocted in ways now known only to old-fashioned schoolmasters. For an insult offered to an alderman the sentence on one defendant was that:

between the eighth and ninth hour, before dinner, with his head uncovered and attended by an officer of the City, should carry a lighted wax candle, weighing two pounds, through Walbrook, Bucklersbury, and so by the Conduit and Chepe, to St Lawrence Lane in the Old Jewry, and along that Lane to the Chapel of the Guildhall aforesaid, and there make offering of the said candle, which done, all further imprisonment was to be remitted to him, and forgiven.

An apparent act of contrite piety, but in truth simply a way to force an offender to make a fool of himself.

Anyone held by the authorities was likely to be paraded through the streets with similar ceremony unless there was a real risk of riot or rescue attempt. Captives did not duck under concealing raincoats, but walked to the cries of the crowd, perhaps with officially-ordered music ringing in their ears, like the adulterers taken to the Tun.

Fines

Throughout history, fines have been popular with the authorities. It may be useful to imprison or execute an important political rival or a thoroughly wicked prisoner, but how much better to enforce the law and show a profit.

In Anglo-Saxon times fines could be imposed for even the most serious crimes, including murder, with the aim both of punishment and of securing compensation for the victims of their families. By the middle of the thirteenth century it was estimated that as much as one-sixth of the king's revenue was gained from fines. Income from offenders may in fact have been much more, since it was also common to seize the assets of felons, and to sell pardons.

Kings appear to have demanded relatively small sums most of the time, well tuned to the ability of the offender to pay. It was even possible to buy in advance pardons for offences yet to be committed, rather like investing in a season ticket, and bargain price pardons were sometimes sold as a limited offer to boost the royal cashflow: for 16s. 4d. (about 82p) a multi-purpose pardon was a prudent purchase, which might not protect against a major prosecution, but would work out cheaper than fines.

Whipping

This was another punishment with the virtue of cheapness, and might be imposed on its own or in conjunction with other punishments. To be 'whipped at a cart's tail' was to be roped to the back of a wagon and, stripped to the waist, receive lashes all along a prescribed route, perhaps past the scene of the crime. Certainly the length of the trip was a measure of the seriousness of the offence. A swifter, less elaborate punishment was to be whipped at the post which each parish maintained.

The methodical chastisement of vagrants taken into Bridewell was a regular public spectacle, and could also be applied as the sentence of a court.

> The manner of whipping there is to strip the party to the skin from the waist upwards, and having fastened him to the whipping-post, so that he can neither resist nor shun the strokes, to lash the naked body with long but slender twigs of holly, which now bend almost like thongs and lap around the body, and these have little knots upon them, tear the skin and flesh, and give extreme pain.

This was Thomas Elwood's account of whippings at Bridewell, where he and several other Quakers were sent for their views. Ironically, the integrity of Quakers was held in such regard that they were sent from the Sessions House without an escort, as they had promised to go straight to the prison.

Whipping in prison was not confined to Bridewell, and lasted until 1967 as a punishment for prison indiscipline. However, while prisons were poorly run, formal flogging was rare; it took the well-regulated reforming regime of the penitentiary system to make whipping both regular and savage. One zealot was incensed when a prisoner at Millbank had his sentence of 100 lashes halved, and wrote: 'Were proof required of the exceeding mildness of the rule under which Millbank was governed we should have it here. But, really, all milk-and-water tenderness is misplaced in the management of criminals.' For most of the nineteenth century corporal punishment, which had been so common as hardly to attract comment in previous times, was the subject of intricate debate and negotiation. By the 1830s many courts sentenced offenders to be whipped, yet left the nature and severity of the punishment to the governor of the prison to decide; when it became mandatory to specify the maximum number of strokes to be inflicted, governors still had to exercise their discretion, since the numbers of lashes were often so high as to kill or maim.

An outbreak of 'garotting' – street robbery using a stranglehold, though rarely to the point of killing – drew a predictable call, in the mid-Victorian years, for severe physical punishment. In fact, although many claimed that flogging ended the fashion for garotting, there was a steady tendency to reduce the number of floggings (which like hangings were removed from view within the prison walls) and to regulate their severity. They became rarities as sentences and as prison disciplinary punishments, with governors proud to point out that their management of prisons was such as to avoid recourse to the whip.

Although still available for prison discipline into the 1960s, flogging and birching were abolished as court sentences in 1948. Birching, most commonly used for young offenders, had been strokes of a thin cane on the bare buttocks, usually performed in a police station or within a court building. Canes of differing lengths and weights were prescribed for the under-tens, over-tens and adults. Flogging was with a cat-o'-nine-tails, of cords attached to a handle, applied across the bare back in prisons. Both in absolute numbers, and in the proportion of cases in which they were used, both birching and

flogging had largely fallen into disuse long before they
were abolished. Those who call for their reintroduction
rarely recall that these were punishments abandoned by
conservative courts long before they were abolished by
liberal-minded politicians.

Branding

Branding was a survival from Anglo-Saxon times. It was
a versatile punishment, combining immediate pain with
a permanent visible record of a conviction – significant
for those offences carrying the death penalty for a second
offence. The brand also served as a warning to strangers
in their dealings with a convicted criminal.

Elaborate codes were developed, some recognized in
law, others local inventions. The 1547 Statute of Vagabonds established the brand V for runaway servants,
to which S (Slave) was added for any further escapes.
F marked the Fraymaker or brawler, especially if the
offence had been in a church, in which case an ear was
to be removed. B stood for Blasphemer, though this
might mean no more than holding unpopular beliefs,
and was applied to the forehead, while SL on a cheek
meant Seditious Libel, SS meant Sower of Sedition. K
might be burned in for treasonable remarks, T for thief,
M for malefactor or manslaughter; FA was the mark of the
False Accuser. Each of these might be applied to the hand,
wrist or other visible spot. A deserter from the army might
carry D in the left armpit, a soldier of Bad Character BC,
but these were tattoos of ink and gunpowder rather than
hot brands.

Branding was often an addition to other penalties, but
a bribe could well result in a cold iron being applied, and
a visitor to London in 1710 watched as petty offenders
were officially cold-ironed: they were not told what was
to happen, and 'set up a great screaming' until it became

clear that the iron had been drawn from the ground, not the fire!

Later, in a form of Benefit of Clergy, those who could read might pay 13½ pence to have the iron quenched before it was applied. Civil courts did not sentence to branding after 1829, though military tattooing was used until 1858. The legal system is often slow to strike a penalty from the statute books, and final abolition had to wait until 1879.

Mutilation

We are swift to criticize other countries in which scriptural authority is used to justify mutilation, but exactly the same practices were common in England. Tongues that had uttered slanders or treasons were cut out, hands that had stolen or assaulted severed at a blow. Feet were cut off to help prevent further offending. Ears were nailed to pillories, and if the victim did not tear himself free, the ear would be slit or severed; nose-slitting was a common addition to other punishments, and was favoured for prostitutes, perhaps with the intent of damaging their trade. By the end of the eighteenth century most courts were content to limit physical punishment to a flogging.

The Pillory

> The Curls of his Wig were so pasted and matted
> Allover so daub'd, so beplumbed and befatted
> So Eggy withal, that a Man would have sworn,
> He had just in the Pill'ry been taking a turn.
>
> from *The Rambling Fuddle-Caps;*
> *or a Tavern Struggle for a Kiss*, written in 1709
> by Ned Ward, himself twice pilloried, at the Royal
> Exchange and Charing Cross

Combining public humiliation with discomfort and the

chance for people to express their feelings about an
offender, display in the pillory was a common punishment
for hundreds of years. There were pillories at many points
throughout London – an upright post, perhaps raised on a
platform, bearing a hinged pair of planks with holes for
hands and neck.

When London was small, exposure in the pillory seems
to have worked well in warning the public about dishonest
tradesmen. In 1269 the pillory in Cheapside was broken,
and went unrepaired for more than a year. The local bakers
had been regularly placed in the pillory and it is recorded
that during that year the weight of an average loaf fell by
more than one third, to rise again only when the pillory
was restored.

The crime of the culprit was often shouted to the
crowd, or some evidence of the offence placed for all to
see. Shoddy goods might be hung like a garland over the
pillory itself, or a note pinned to the offender's cap. When
William Bowyer was sentenced in 1391 for forging a false
deed, the sentence was that he:

On the Monday next ensuing, between the hours of 10 and 11
before noon, with bare head and bare feet, should be put upon
the pillory, there to remain for one hour of the day, the said
false deed being hung about his neck; and that he should from
thence be taken back to prison; and so on the Wednesday and
Friday after, at the same hour, be again put on the pillory, for
one hour each day; and that each time the cause thereof should
be proclaimed.

Bowyer was also barred from public office, barred from
trading, and 'should be held and reputed for the future as
one defamed, false, and infamous' – the pillory offered a
chance for all to identify him, as effective as a front-page
photograph.

We do not know how Bowyer was treated during his three hours in the pillory, but we do know that this was a punishment in which the authorities and public both took a hand. There was great sport to be had in throwing eggs, vegetables, dead cats, dogs, rats and mice at the helpless culprit, but the crowd could also be kind. When Defoe was pilloried at Temple Bar for publishing a pamphlet which displeased the High Court party of the time, the crowd drank to his health, placed flowers around his head, and sang a verse from Defoe's own *Hymn to the Pillory*:

> Tell them the men who placed him here
>   Are scandals to the times:
> Are at a loss to find his guilt,
>   And can't commit his crimes.

To make the punishment fit the crime, dishonest tradesmen would be pelted with their own produce, or have it burned beneath their noses. More seriously, offenders who aroused real anger were at risk of their lives, when stones replaced messier missiles. Deaths were not uncommon, and a prudent person might go to the pillory with protection. In 1680 one Elizabeth Cellier was in danger from extreme Protestants and was allowed a chair and a wooden shield; a man pilloried in Southwark for perjury which had caused an innocent man to hang was lucky to escape with his life – 'But, tho' he had a Tin Scull-Plate under his Cap, he was cut in the left side of the head.'

Only slowly did the pillory fall from favour, to be abolished in 1837.

SIR THOMAS DE TURBERVILLE (1295)

Sir Thomas had been captured by the French, and turned traitor. We have a detailed and chilling description of his public humiliation, trial and execution which shows how much importance was given to the public theatre of justice and punishment.

He came from the Tower, mounted on a poor hack, in a coat of ray [rayed, or striped cloth], and shod with white shoes, his head being covered with a hood, and his feet tied beneath the horse's belly, and his hands tied before him: and around him were riding six torturers attired in the form of the devil, one of whom held his rein, and the hangman his halter, for the horse which bore him had them both upon it: and in such a manner was he led from the Tower through London to Westminster, and was condemned on the dais in the Great Hall there; and Sir Roger Brabazun pronounced judgement upon him, that he should be drawn and hanged, and that he should hang so long as anything be left whole of him; and he was drawn on a fresh ox-hide from Westminster to the Conduit of London [in Cheapside] and then back to the gallows [probably the Elms, in West Smithfield]; and there he is hung by a chain of iron, and will hang, so long as anything of him may remain.

The journeys across London, for a total of more than seven miles, must have given almost every Londoner a chance to revile the traitor, but also to be awed by a show calculated to frighten and deter.

EXECUTION

William the Conqueror abolished capital punishment. Under Saxon and Danish rule offenders had been put to death by hanging and drowning but the Normans brought with them a code which replaced killing with mutilation. William's motives may not have been entirely philanthropic – the right to execute had been a privilege of the barons from whom he wished to strip power. Nor were the substitute penalties lenient, with blinding particularly favoured.

Although prohibiting common execution, the king nonetheless reserved the right to put his political opponents to death, and just ten years after the Conquest was the first beheading, of the Earl of Huntingdon, Northampton and Northumberland. This was considered an honourable death by the Normans, and according to their custom, was performed with a sword. Like many of the new regime's institutions, beheading retained its courtly status over the coarser native practice of hanging.

Steadily, capital punishment returned. Killing a criminal achieved many ends simply and cheaply: the permanent removal of an offender who might commit further crimes at a time when the prisons did not exist in which offenders could be detained in great numbers for long periods; the public expression of the power of the king's courts; and some deterrent effect when the lack of any systematic law enforcement made capture and conviction a lottery.

For maximum effect there had to be maximum ceremony. The death was the climax to a prolonged public
display in which the power of authority and the wretchedness of the captive were acted out in a procession which
every citizen might see.

Hanging became the standard punishment for ordinary
criminals, beheading for the nobility. Drowning had once
been a common way of executing women – the baronial
right of 'pit and gallows' gave power to execute both sexes
– but seems never to have returned as an official ritual.

Burning came to be used for ideological and religious
offences, from witchcraft to heresy, perhaps because it
was more symbolic of the destruction of the evil within
a person, not merely the life. For a fee, many hangmen
would strangle, or at least choke into unconsciousness,
the victim at the stake, although there were examples of
executioners insufficiently bribed, or too incompetent, to
achieve this. Burning was also regarded as a more fitting
and decorous alternative for women when the prescribed
punishment was hanging, drawing and quartering.

Men sentenced to be hanged, drawn and quartered were
first drawn to the site of execution behind a horse or a
cart. At first the condemned were simply dragged along
the ground, but many failed to survive; later victims were
placed on hurdles or hides. They were then hanged, but
while still alive, often fully conscious, would be lowered
to the ground and castrated. Disembowelment, and the
burning of the viscera, would be performed before the
victim's eyes, and only then would they be decapitated.
The body would be quartered, and to make sure that
head and quarters would be preserved for exhibition,
they would be boiled in a prepared cauldron, and might
be coated in pitch.

Time after time this bloody hacking was performed on

traitors and those who had merely fallen from favour, to the delight of a knowing crowd. Not until 1814 was the punishment reduced to simple hanging, with decapitation after death, and although unused after 1820, even this remained on the statute books until 1870. Other forms of execution were decreed for specific offences: poisoners might be boiled (*see* Smithfield), and military prisoners executed by shooting in Hyde Park or at the Tower, but these were much less common events than the regular extermination at Smithfield and Tyburn by rope and stake.

Each single death had grotesque fascination for the spectators. What must also be remembered is the prodigious numbers of executions carried out. One estimate has it that during the thirty-eight-year reign of Henry VIII about 72,000 were put to death: to judge how commonplace public execution had become, this figure is equivalent to the public killing of 20,000 people each year in the larger population of twentieth-century Britain.

In each generation additional offences were made punishable by death, but in the early eighteenth century a quite extraordinary range of misdeeds were added to the list, most notoriously by the Waltham Black Act of 1722, which was intended as temporary legislation to meet an outbreak of lawlessness in Hampshire, but became the basis for a code which prescribed death for bizarrely inconsequential offences such as writing on Westminster Bridge.

It must not be thought that the number of executions rose dramatically. The statutes, which came to list more than 200 capital offences, became a catalogue of the fears of the property-owning classes, yet juries faced with a wretched trivial offender were reluctant to convict even where the evidence was glaring. Pardons, and commutations to transportation, became so common that, of those condemned, only one in seven would go to Tyburn.

In time, of course, the excesses of the law came to defeat their own purpose. If deterrence was based on the certainty of discovery, capture, conviction and punishment, it could not operate for as long as each stage was a lottery. Despite the efforts of juries, children and the most minor and pitiful offenders went to the gallows, to the discredit of the entire system of justice, and by the nineteenth century there was a sense of shame even among conservative and traditional citizens. In 1830 Sir Robert Peel said in Parliament: 'It is impossible to conceal from ourselves that capital punishments are more frequent and the criminal law more severe on the whole in this country than in any country in the world.'

The British tend to confuse questions of morality and good taste. For more than two generations, from the end of the eighteenth to the middle of the nineteenth centuries, there was little agreement about capital punishment, between those who were properly offended by the rituals of public execution and those troubled by the laws which condemned so many. While other countries examined carefully the necessity of putting criminals to death, British reformers succeeded merely in abolishing the progress to Tyburn; while others reduced the number of offences for which death might be a penalty, British governments relied on pardons and commutations to keep the figures of those hanged acceptably low. In three years – 1827 to 1830 – 451 people were convicted of capital crimes in the London area, and of them 55 were hanged.

From 1830 serious attempts, led by Peel, were made to reduce the number of capital crimes, and total abolition might have followed had not the focus again shifted to the propriety of public execution, which was abolished in 1868 against the opposition of those who still placed their faith in the deterrent effect of spectacle.

The very practice and method of execution had also changed. Satisfaction at the suffering of the dying was replaced by pity and a concern to make death swift and dignified. Executioners began to take a pride in their craftsmanship (*see* The Hangmen), and the procedure was shortened from the hours taken in travelling to Tyburn to the twenty seconds claimed by Pierrepoint for a well-conducted modern execution. First the scaffold was moved across town, to stand outside (or atop, in the case of Horsemonger Lane) the prison, then to within the walls. The final development was to create a suite in which the condemned cell was adjacent to the drop. There came to be no last walk, no climb to the scaffold; the closeness of the scaffold was concealed from the prisoner, who would find himself conducted swiftly through a door previously disguised and concealed, to stand only briefly on the trapdoors. Only one such scaffold still exists in Britain, at Wandsworth, against the possibility that a conviction for the only remaining capital crime, treason, or a more general restoration of hanging, might bring it back into use.

BENEFIT OF CLERGY

When there were two systems of law, of the Church and of the king, anyone in holy orders had a notable privilege. If accused of a felony – a crime which carried the death sentence – he or she could establish their religious status, plead 'benefit of clergy' and avoid execution. Sentence was then a matter for an ecclesiastical court, and the customary sentence in such cases was one year's imprisonment, in the custody of the local bishop rather than in a common gaol.

At a time when few but the clergy could read or write, a simple test was applied to determine whether a defendant was a clerk in holy orders: he or she would be called on to read a verse from the Bible. The same verse was always used, the first in the Fifty-First Psalm: 'Have mercy on me, O God, according to Thy steadfast love; according to Thy abundant mercy blot out my transgressions.' It was intended that the privilege should be used only once, and many defendants were branded on the palm or thumb to prevent further claims.

The benefit was widely abused. The use of the single 'neck verse' made it an easy matter for an illiterate person to be coached in memorizing it, and it could be arranged, for a fee, that the branding iron would be applied cold. One result of benefit of clergy was the increased use of prisons, as 'clerks' who had cheated the gallows went to gaol instead.

SMITHFIELD

Smithfield (from 'smooth field') was a place for trading and pleasure beyond the City walls to the north. It was the venue of Bartholomew Fair, the great market and carnival which raised money each year for the hospital nearby, with every kind of amusement and sideshow.

For four hundred years it was also a place of execution. Prisoners were taken to the Elms, perhaps at first to be hanged from the trees themselves, although there was certainly a gallows 'betwixt the horse pool and the river of Wel'. The pool may well have been that used for execution; the river was the Fleet, which traced through an area with many springs and wells.

In 1196 a congregation of Satanists was found in devil-worship in the church of St Mary-le-Bow in Cheapside, their ritual led by one William FitzOsbert. Besieged in the church, they were finally captured and taken to Smithfield to hang, calling on the Devil to rescue them. Another account, however, pointed out that FitzOsbert had made a public protest at St Paul's against unfair taxation which had angered the authorities. The Satanism version of events has about it a familiar smell of official disinformation.

The most famous of the early executions was the hanging and quartering of William Wallace, the Scottish patriot and guerilla leader who had resisted the English for thirty years. In 1305 he was captured and brought to London, and following execution his was the first head to be exhibited on London Bridge. From Smithfield the quarters of his body went further afield to be put on show in Newcastle, Berwick, Perth and Stirling.

In 1349 the bodies of tens of thousands of victims of the Black Death were cast into pits in Smithfield, and it was here that the Peasants' Revolt of 1381 was halted. Throughout their campaign the rebels of Kent and Essex had believed that their oppressors were the nobles and rich clergy, and that Richard II could and would help them. The young King met them at Smithfield, but on a pretext William Walworth, Mayor of London, struck down Wat Tyler, the rebels' leader. Wounded, Tyler took refuge in the church of St Bartholomew, but was dragged out and beheaded. Richard, though only fourteen years old, had the presence of mind to address the insurgents, convincing them that he would be their champion. Confused, but trusting that their grievances would now be heard and answered, the rebels dispersed. During the next weeks they were hunted down and their leaders exterminated.

The 1450 rebellion of Jack Cade also reached Smithfield – Shakespeare includes a scene set there in *Henry VI Part Two*, and in the same play is a squalid example of 'trial by

battle'. On the assumption that God would grant victory
to the good and the innocent, such trials were no more
than a fight, often to the death. Smithfield was commonly
used for the combats, and long after the law had forbidden
the trials, duellists took their quarrels to the field near the
Elms.

In 1530 a new and terrible punishment for poisoners was
inflicted here for the first time. The cook to the Bishop
of Lancaster, one Richard Rose, had attempted to murder
his master by poisoning a quantity of yeast. The bishop
survived, but seventeen others died, and a new sentence
was prescribed for the poisoners of masters and spouses
– boiling alive. Rose was placed in a huge iron cauldron
slung from a tripod over a log pile, and died two hours
after the fire was lit. A little clemency was shown to later
poisoners, and the water or oil was brought to boiling
before the culprit was thrown in.

'The witch in Smithfield shall be burned to ashes . . . '
This line, again from *Henry VI*, points to the use of
Smithfield as the place where witches, heretics and
religious opponents were burned at the stake. It was
associated in particular with the Protestant martyrdoms
of Tudor times, of which Foxe gave highly imaginative
accounts in his *Book of Martyrs*. Extracts from this are still
in print more than 400 years later to keep the memory of
the martyrs alive among those in fear of Popish plots. We
do know that Mary Tudor sent forty-three of her religious
opponents to their death here, and in 1849 builders
unearthed a large quantity of charred human remains,
and what appeared to be a stake still bearing the iron
collar used to hold the condemned. It had been recorded
that those to be burned were made to face the west door
of the church of St Bartholomew the Great, and it was
just there that the grim relics were found.

The inevitable Protestant revenge was taken, though

most commonly at Tyburn. Smithfield's use for executions declined, and the area degenerated into the haunt of ruffians and duellists. In 1615 the area was drained, paved and fenced, and a cattle market established in 1638. When the problems of moving livestock and coping with the slaughterhouses became too much in the nineteenth century, the market was limited to meat, and as such has continued to this day.

The Site Now

The meat market occupies most of the old broad field, but the area before the remaining gate of St Bartholomew's – the scene of executions – remains open. A plaque records the death of William Wallace, and on the wall of St Bartholomew's Hospital is a tablet commemorating John Rogers, first of London's Protestant martyrs.

TYBURN

From the twelfth century until 1783 condemned prisoners were led, dragged and carried to a spot well to the west of London to be put to death. No accurate total of executions can be reached, but probably more than 60,000 people died close to the present junction at Marble Arch.

We cannot know why the site was chosen, except that it stood at the junction of three important roads, well away from both the City and Westminster, amid fields broad enough to hold large crowds. Perhaps in the earliest times there was a particularly prominent and suitable tree or trees. Gallows were stored locally and erected for each execution until in 1571 the infamous Triple Tree was erected. This was London's first permanent gallows, of a size and shape to permit the hanging of many people at a time. Three tall posts, eighteen feet high, were connected by crossbeams nine feet long, each capable of holding eight victims. We know of only one occasion when the full capacity was reached, and twenty-four people were hanged together in 1649, but multiple executions were the rule rather than the exception.

Although it had been used earlier on occasion, Tyburn had eclipsed Smithfield and St Giles (by the end of the fourteenth century) as the principal place for London's executions, and a lengthy ritual was established in which prisoners rode to the gallows from Newgate and occasionally the Tower.

During the time between the sentence and the execution – at first as little as a week – word would spread about the crime and the criminal. Broadsheets and pamphlets fed and reinforced gossip, and many sightseers would pay the turnkeys at Newgate to take a look at the condemned prisoners, either in the Condemned Hold or during the last service for the condemned (*see* Newgate). In these last days some of the prisoners spent time in reflection and spiritual preparation, but many others passed the days in boisterous entertaining, with friends and family invited to join in feasting, drinking, even dancing.

On the last evening the final sacrament would be offered, and at midnight a bell was rung to accompany the chanting of a plea to the condemned. This stage in the ritual was created by a bequest to St Sepulchre's, the church nearest to Newgate: £50 was provided annually for the bellman to pronounce 'solemnly two exhortations to the persons condemned'. On that night before the execution, the cry would rise:

> All you that in the condemned hole do lie,
> Prepare you, for tomorrow you shall die;
> Watch all and pray; The hour is drawing near,
> That you before the Almighty must appear.
>
> Examine well yourselves; in time repent,
> That you may not to eternal flames be sent.

And when St Sepulchre's Bell in the morning tolls,
The Lord above have mercy on your souls.

On the following morning, in states of confusion, terror
and probably hangover, the prisoners were taken to the
Press Room, their irons struck off and replaced by a cord
to bind their arms, and a halter placed about their necks.
The choice of clothes was left to the prisoner; some chose
to die in their finest, others wore shrouds as a sign of
repentance. There were also those who, knowing that
their clothing would be claimed by the hangman, wore
a simple cheap garment such as a nightshirt, to cheat him
of his profit.

Traitors were once dragged at a horse's tail as part of
their punishment, and to increase their discomfort still
further stones might be thrown into their path, but so
many failed to survive the journey that a hide was put
under them as protection, and later a hurdle as a simple
sled. Common criminals were usually loaded into wide
carts, but those who had carriages were allowed to travel
in them, even offering lifts to their fellow-condemned,
and from time to time a prisoner would hire an elaborate
carriage for the occasion to make a grand exit.

The Road to Tyburn

As clever Tom Clinch, while the Rabble was bawling,
Rode stately through Holbourn to die in his Calling;
He stopt at the George for a Bottle of Sack,
And promis'd to pay for it when he'd come back.

His Waistcoat, and Stockings, and Breeches were white,
His Cap had a new Cherry Ribbon to ty't;
The Maids to the Doors and the Balconies ran,
And said, Lack-a-day! he's a proper young Man!

Clever Tom Clinch going to be Hanged, Swift (1727)

After the second address from the St Sepulchre's bellman, the procession would set off. An escort accompanied the carts, led by the City Marshal, and Under Marshal, who had command of marshalmen, javelin men and constables, in whatever strength was thought necessary for crowd control along the route: they had to force a way through drunken mobs, thwart rescue attempts, or protect prisoners from lynching until they could be lawfully hanged, and the task would commonly require 200 men. If a traitor were being drawn on a hurdle, sheriff's officers rode with him, sabres drawn.

The hangman would ride in one of the leading carts, to arrive early and make preparations, though on one occasion in the eighteenth century the hangman was arrested en route on a warrant for debt, and his prisoners had to be returned to Newgate, where they were pardoned. A chaplain would ride in one of the carts with the condemned, who might also be joined by family or friends.

Hanging days were public holidays, and the route would be lined with Londoners eating, drinking, and hoping for lively action. 'All the Way, from Newgate to Tyburn, is one continued fair, for Whores and Rogues of the meaner Sort.' A popular prisoner might treat the journey as a last chance to bask in the admiration of his public: 'The day appointed by law for the thief's shame is the day of glory in his own opinion. His procession to Tyburn and his last moments there are all triumphant. . . .' But a prisoner hated by the crowd could expect to be abused, and to have stones, excrement, even dead animals hurled at him.

The carts could move only slowly along Holborn to Tyburn Road (now Oxford Street), and at taverns and alehouses along the way the condemned could eat and drink as much as he chose. The standard joke, as Swift recorded, was that the bill would be paid on the way back, and in the three hours which the journey might take, the account would have been considerable.

At Tyburn

Around the gallows a crowd would already have gathered at the food and drink stalls, or to make sure of a seat in the large grandstand erected there in 1724. The stand, known as Mother Proctor's Pews after the owner, was a valuable property, with takings said to have reached £5,000 when Earl Ferrers was hanged in 1760.

The crowd which had followed the procession would arrive to congest the area around the gallows still further, and the tension would mount as preparations were completed.

At first prisoners were forced to mount a ladder, their nooses hitched to a crossbar, and they were then to throw themselves off. If they failed to do this, they were pushed from the ladder or 'turned off', an expression that remained in the language for as long as capital punishment was retained. Later, prisoners stood at the tail of the cart and the horses were lashed to pull the cart from under their feet. Before this a quarter of an hour or more might have passed as all the prisoners bade farewell to their families and friends, were consoled by clergy, gave and received gifts, and of course made speeches. The hangman and any assistants would pass among the condemned to secure any who had arrived unbound, to place nooses around necks, and cover faces with cloths or bags when this had become the practice. Prisoners commonly gave the hangman money, hoping to make sure of a quick end, and might arrange a signal which would tell him that they were ready to die, such as a wave of the hand or the dropping of a kerchief.

When all was ready, the cart would go, and the

condemned would strangle. To speed the death, friends might hang on the victims' legs or beat their chests with stones. The hangman might help, and would also try to ensure that no one was being lifted in an attempt to save them. After a struggle that might last a quarter of an hour, life would be gone.

Throughout all this the crowd would comment on the proceedings. They were used to the sight of hangings and like knowledgeable spectators at a bullfight would shout opinions of the skill of the executioner. A late reprieve might cause jubilation, or cause a riot. The crowd was aware that a cat-and-mouse game was played with the condemned in which reprieve was delayed until the last minute, even to the point of allowing a traitor to be half-hanged, cut down and marked out for quartering before being told he was to be spared. This added to the terror of prisoners and the tension of the crowd; in the hope of such a reprieve farewell speeches were often long enough to annoy a restive crowd.

Spectators looked for signs of drunkenness, clumsiness or incompetence in the hangman, and if he made a particularly bad job of it he might be forced to flee. With both prisoners and hangmen the worse for drink, brawls on the cart were common, and on one occasion force had to be used to prevent the execution of a chaplain. The hangman had strung three nooses, and not having been told of an earlier reprieve for one man, was drunkenly sure that all three men on his cart must hang!

Death itself held no surprises and few horrors for the crowd: 'There is nothing in being hanged but a wry Neck, and a wet pair of Breeches.'

THE HANGMEN

As famous as actors and princes in their time (though often more reviled than the criminals they flogged and put to death), the hangmen were until the last century a slovenly, incompetent and criminal bunch. The first executioner on record was not named, but was identified by his stump leg. He beheaded the Duke of Northumberland on Tower Hill, but was later hanged himself at Tyburn, and several of his successors met the same ironic fate. At least two escaped the rope only by offering to execute others, most notoriously Edward Dennis, who was condemned for his part in the Gordon Riots, and asked that his son be appointed hangman in his stead. Perhaps the thought of son hanging father was too much – Dennis was released to execute thirty-four of his fellow-rioters.

The most famous executioner of the seventeenth century was Jack Ketch, whose name came to be applied to all hangmen after he had dispatched more than 200 rebel followers of the Duke of Monmouth, and then made a clumsy, prolonged mess of cutting off the head of Monmouth himself. Another whose name entered the language was Derrick, an unsavoury man who was condemned for rape, reprieved at the request of the Earl of Essex, yet beheaded Essex some years later. It has been suggested that Derrick winched up his victims on a device which would give its name to a crane, but there is no record of such a contraption; the name was probably simple gallows humour.

The removal of hangings from Tyburn to Newgate was intended to make executions more respectable, and although the sheriffs chose less seedy

hangmen, their competence was as questionable as
ever. There had been little skill in throwing victims
from ladders or whipping a horse to drag away a
cart, but the introduction of a scaffold with a drop
meant that there was more to go wrong. Calcraft,
the most famous of the nineteenth-century hangmen,
served for forty-five years and retired at the age of
seventy-four. As a man he seems to have been gentle,
absorbed in his trade as a cobbler, and in his hobbies
of gardening and breeding prize rabbits, but as an
executioner he was appalling. He persisted in using
a traditional short drop of just a couple of feet, which
damned his victims to slow strangulation instead of
the quick end which the trapdoor was intended to
provide. If death took too long even for Calcraft he
would climb upon the back of the hanging body, or
drag on its feet. His manner and appearance were
far from solemn. 'I must keep my client in good
spirits. Besides I am not a parson or an undertaker,
and therefore decline to don funeral garments.' The
crowd usually loathed him, and Dickens spoke for
many when he observed that 'Mr Calcraft should be
restrained in his unseemly briskness, in his jokes, his
oaths and his brandy'.

Calcraft's more dignified and scientific successor,
Marwood, was the first to calculate drops which
would guarantee swift and merciful death, setting
standards which most of his successors would follow.
There had been several examples of fathers following
sons in the calling of executioner, and among the
last of Britain's hangmen were three members of
the Pierrepoint family – Henry, his brother Thomas,
and Henry's son Albert, who served more than
half a century between them. Albert Pierrepoint's
autobiography is by far the best account of this

strange profession: it is thoughtful and far from
sensationalist. Having hanged many hundreds, he
explains carefully his conclusion that capital punishment is worthless as a deterrent, and should be
universally abolished.

After the Hanging

Events at Tyburn did not end with the death of the victim.
He might already have paid an undertaker who would be
on hand to take the body for burial. Poorer prisoners
would be taken away by the authorities, and buried close
by, or their bodies given to their families. Arguments
about clothing and possessions were common, and even
more heated were battles over bodies.

The anatomists who trained surgeons were allowed a
legal quota of just ten bodies each year from among the
hanged, but would pay very good money to anyone who
could bring in more. There was enormous revulsion
against dissectionists, and the crowd would join families
in fighting off anyone who tried to make off with a body.
Families might also have hired a physician to be on hand
in the hope of reviving a victim, and would be in haste
to take the body away.

Adding to the chaos were those who believed in the
curative properties of the bodies, who paid hangmen for
the chance to press a dead hand to an infection or injury,
even trying to take hair, blood or parts of the body. The
superstitions extended to the rope used, and hangmen
would sell pieces of rope to the clamouring crowd.

These foul scenes were repeated many times in a year,
and the crowds might reach 100,000. Revulsion against the
disorder and squalor of the proceedings was eventually
strong enough to force a change. Camden Town was at
first suggested, for a fresh start, but in 1783 it was decided
to move the gallows to Newgate.

Just to the south of the gallows, in Hyde Park, was the spot where military executions were held. Mutineers and other offenders against army discipline faced a firing squad here.

The Site Now

There is a plaque set into the footway on the traffic island at Marble Arch, but a more probable site for the gallows is a few paces up the Edgware Road, on the western side close to the corner of Connaught Place. The military executions were at or close to the concrete-covered area at Speaker's Corner.

OTHER SITES OF EXECUTION

In 1281 the Abbot of Westminster had gallows at Westminster, Teddington, Knightsbridge, Greenford, Chelsea, Brentford, Paddington, Iveney, Laleham, Hampstead, Ecclesford, Staines, Halliford, Westbourne and Shepperton.

The English gained notoriety for their readiness to hang their fellows. No other nation seemed so eager to condemn offenders to death for minor offences, so unwilling to pardon or contemplate less drastic punishment. Just as England is notable today for the numbers committed to prison, so it was held remarkable for the numbers put to death.

Smithfield and Tyburn saw victims die in their tens of thousands, but across London many other places were used, once or regularly, for executions. Any prominent or busy place might have a gallows, placed as a steady reminder to the people, or the executions held close to the scene of a crime. Only the delicacy of more recent years has changed the names of the Gallows Places once found across the map of London.

There can be no comprehensive list, nor can many of the sites be identified precisely where the line of a road has changed, or the area completely redeveloped. Further complications arise in distinguishing those places used for executions, and the sites of gibbets used to display bodies, or parts of bodies, brought and left hanging as a public warning. Legends may not always be reliable: some believe that the altar of Westminster Cathedral stands on the site of a gallows within a prison. Tothill Fields Prison certainly occupied the Cathedral site, but had no gallows.

The City

Those who believed, despite the evidence of their own lawless times, that public execution would be a deterrent, were often further taken by the idea that an offender should be punished at the scene of the crime, to impress upon the neighbourhood the force of law and the grimness of retribution. Hangings and burnings were stage-managed in convenient open spaces, with the practical advantage that it was easier to convey a prisoner short distances within the City when there was a risk of rescue attempt or mob disorder.

In 1517, following a major riot incited by a preacher, in which apprentices, clerics and others attacked the businesses and homes of foreign merchants and craftsmen, gallows were set up at many of the scenes of incidents during the riots: Aldgate, Blanchappleton, Gracechurch Street, Leadenhall, before the Counters and Newgate, St Martin's, Aldersgate, and Bishopsgate. Although hundreds had been held and faced hanging, just thirteen had been executed when Wolsey interceded with the King on behalf of the remainder, who were spared.

In 1595, when popular unrest was feared again, the Provost Marshal of the City was given a portable gallows

on which he might summarily hang the troublesome. The
historian John Stow, living in Aldgate, was able to make
a faithful record of one man's last words with ease – the
gallows had been placed on the pavement outside Stow's
own house.

Not all hangings were so impromptu. There was time
for a crowd of at least 12,000 spectators to gather in
Leadenhall for the execution of Colonel Turner, who spent
half an hour on his final speech – probably hoping for a
reprieve – and incensed the crowd by his tactics. He also
caused great discomfort to Pepys, who noted that having
paid a shilling to stand on a cart-wheel to get a better view,
he developed cramp while Turner played for time.

In Cheapside, by the church of St Mary-le-Bow, where
the leader of the Evil May Day riot had been hanged, stood
a fountain known as the Standard, and as a landmark was
often chosen for hangings and beheadings.

Along the north side of the old St Paul's Cathedral ran a
street – St Paul's Churchyard – which was the centre of the
book trade, and the scene of executions during the Tudor
religious persecutions, and here some of those implicated
in the Gunpowder Plot were executed in 1606.

Along the Thames

Just as gallows and gibbets were erected to impress those
approaching London by land, so down the river were
places of execution chosen to awe those arriving by water.

It is difficult now to imagine how dependent upon river
traffic London once was. For centuries the only bridge
was London Bridge, and most people, and their goods,
crossed by boat. The river was used to bring supplies to
and from London and from settlements upstream. The
traffic attracted its own criminals, from sneak thieves as
skilled as their burgling brothers ashore, to bold gangs
of pirates who would seize a cargo in broad daylight.

These pirates were not as romantic as the tropical figures of *Treasure Island*, but their plunder was enormous, losses to them running to hundreds of thousands of pounds each year in the sixteenth and seventeenth centuries.

The sentence for convicted pirates was that they should hang 'until three tides had overflowed them', and this is often taken to mean that the victims were drowned. Some early offenders may have been weighted and thrown into the water, but the sentence almost certainly meant that the gallows would be erected on the foreshore for a conventional hanging, then left in place: three tides would have meant three working shifts of sailors riding the tide to and from London, a large audience. One spot in Wapping was most frequently used, and was known as Execution Dock; from there bodies were transferred to a gibbet further downstream at Bugsby's Hole near Blackwall, to hang as a warning. The riverside garden of the Town of Ramsgate public house looks on to the spot where the gallows once stood.

On the south shore of the Thames in Bermondsey is an inlet which is in fact the mouth of one of London's concealed rivers, the Neckinger. This name was taken from the Devil's Neckinger, later the Neckinger Wharf, which stood on the western side. A neckinger was a neckcloth, and the Devil's Neckinger an ironic name for the halter or noose of the hangings which took place there. The inlet now forms St Saviour's Dock.

West from the City
By the seventeenth century the population of London had spread far beyond the original walls, and between Holborn and the river was housing as dense as the inner wards, and the custom of local execution spread further.

In 1607 a fencing master called Turner was murdered

in Whitefriars by two men hired by Lord Sanquhar, who had lost an eye in swordplay with Turner. Sanquhar was hanged in Westminster, the others in Fleet Street close to the gate of Whitefriars; one oddity was that one of the men was a Scottish gentleman, page to Sanquhar, and by a Scottish custom of the time was hanged from a gallows fully six feet higher than his low-born co-defendant.

During the Civil War, in 1643, two conspirators against the Parliament were executed close to the house where they had plotted, at the Holborn end of Fetter Lane. Both men, Tomkins and Challenor, followed the custom of addressing the crowd from the ladder before being 'turned off' to their deaths.

We know that for the murder of his master one John Hall was executed in 1741 at the end of Katherine Street in the Strand, and the supposition must be that this was close to the scene of the crime – presumably the decision of the trial judge.

To the north, Lincoln's Inn Fields was used from time to time for executions. In 1586 there was a plot, led by Anthony Babington, to assassinate Elizabeth I, then incite a general uprising among Catholics and place Mary, Queen of Scots on the throne. The plotters were captured, and executed 'in the place where they had used to meet and confere of their traitorous practices': Babington was still conscious when taken down and disembowelled, and hearing of this Elizabeth showed unusual clemency in ordering that the other plotters should hang until dead. During her reign at least two Catholic martyrs met their end here.

Nearly one hundred years later, in 1683, many powerful Whigs wished to dethrone Charles II; in what has become known as the Rye House Plot, a small group plotted to assassinate the King as he returned from Newmarket. Implicated in the plot was William, Lord Russell, and convicted of high treason, he was beheaded in Lincoln's Inn Fields.

St Giles, to the west, was a small village around a leper hospital established in 1101 by Matilda, wife of Henry I. It was she who instructed that a drink – 'Cup of Charity' – should be offered to criminals on their way to Tyburn for execution. For some time after Smithfield ceased to be used, St Giles itself was a place of execution: in 1417 Sir John Oldcastle – the model for Shakespeare's Falstaff – was tried at Westminster Hall and brought here to be hanged over a fire. He was a powerful Lollard, a follower of Wycliffe, and as such regarded as a heretic.

The custom of offering refreshment to the condemned continued for as long as carts drove from Newgate to Tyburn, with many inns keen to gain the increased attention and trade. Drury Lane, close to the half-way point in the journey, was a common stop. St Giles itself became a notorious rookery, or criminal slum, and as such was almost completely demolished; one short stretch of St Giles High Street remains in the shadow of Centre Point, the office block which towers over the junction of Oxford Street, Charing Cross Road, and Tottenham Court Road.

Covent Garden, like many an open space in London, has seen riot and disorder, and in Cromwell's time was used for execution. The most remarkable incident concerned three Welsh Royalists who had defended Pembroke Castle. Brought to London, they had been condemned by a court martial, but a reprieve was offered to two, the choice to be made by drawing lots. The prisoners could not bring themselves to do this, and by a custom of the time a child was offered three pieces of paper to hand out. On two was written 'Life Given by God'. The third went to a Colonel Poyer, who died before a firing squad 'like a soldier'.

Deposed by Parliament, King Charles I was condemned

to death after trial at Westminster Hall. On 30 January 1649 he stepped on to a scaffold built up to first-floor level outside the Banqueting Hall in Whitehall. Wearing two shirts so that he might not shiver with cold and appear afraid, he made a short speech and was beheaded with an axe. Two small uncertainties remain. Charles is known to have stepped on to the platform from a first-floor window, but it is likely that this was not part of the surviving building, but of a small lean-to extension to the left of the frontage. The identity of the executioner is also unclear, since he went to great lengths to disguise himself with a wig and false beard as well as the mask, but many believe it was Richard Brandon, the common hangman.

After the Restoration eight of the regicides – those who had ordered the death of the king – were hanged, drawn and quartered at Charing Cross, within sight of the spot where Charles had lost his head, and we know that at least one – Colonel Harrison – was made to face the Banqueting House as sentence was carried out. The site of this scaffold, and of a later pillory, is now covered by the equestrian statue of Charles I.

Further down Whitehall, outside the Palace of Westminster, is Old Palace Yard, now the corner of the Houses of Parliament which is railed and contains the entrance to the Members' underground car park. Here Guy Fawkes and three other Gunpowder Plotters were hanged, drawn and quartered in 1606. It was from a house that they had rented on the south-east of the Yard that they smuggled barrels of gunpowder into the vaults of the Palace of Westminster.

In 1618 Sir Walter Raleigh walked from the Gatehouse to execution in Old Palace Yard. After a career of distinction and favour he had been imprisoned in the Tower by James I for twelve years, on dubious charges of plotting against the King. Fear of public outrage led the authorities to execute him on the Lord Mayor's Day, when sensation-seekers might be drawn to the revels in the City. Raleigh went to the block with dignity, and although his body was taken and buried in the chancel of St Margaret's Church nearby, his widow carried away his head in a cloth bag. She kept it all her life, bequeathing it to her son.

North and South

Executions were carried out in many parts of London, but records are often unhelpful in establishing precise sites. To the north, it is known that Catholic priests were burned in Islington, and that hangings took place north of Islington at what is now the junction of Liverpool Road and Holloway Road. To the west, there was once a plan to use the centre of Camden Town as the principal place of execution: the *Morning Post* reported in 1776 that 'Orders have been given from the Secretary of State's office that the criminals capitally convicted at the Old Bailey shall in future be executed at the crossroad near the "Mother Red Cap" inn, the half-way house to Hampstead, and that no galleries, scaffolds, or other temporary stages be built near the place.' The aim must have been to avoid the outrageous carnival atmosphere of Tyburn and the risks of the journey, but in 1783, when Tyburn ceased to be used, the space in front of Newgate must have been even more convenient than the Camden Town site, which does not appear to have been taken up after all.

On the northern edge of Hampstead Heath, on the road to Hendon, was a gibbet on which the bodies of the highwaymen of the area were displayed, although this may not have been used in their execution. The post of this gibbet was said to have been used later as a mantel-tree over a fireplace in Jack Straw's Castle, the inn at the top of the heath. The site of the gibbet seems to have been just north of the side-road into the pub car park.

Far to the south, the main place of execution in Surrey was Kennington Common, where those convicted at the Court at St Margaret's, in Borough High Street, were put to death. The routes from the local prisons to Kennington were scenes of festivity just like the route to Tyburn, with hot-pie stalls, brandy-sellers, apple-women, and boys selling lurid broadsheets telling the story of the crimes. On days when both Kennington and Tyburn were to hold hangings, spectators considered carefully which event would offer the greater sport.

Among the most famous to suffer at Kennington were the Jacobite rebels, followers of Bonnie Prince Charlie, who were captured and brought south for trial. In a series of spectacles, they were hanged, drawn and quartered at Kennington.

Most of Kennington Common has now been covered by housing, only Kennington Park remaining. The gallows stood on a spot now occupied by St Mark's, the prominent church close to Oval Underground station. The socket in which the upright post of the scaffold once stood was said to have been discovered in the crypt of the church, but on a recent visit I was told that no identifiable evidence remains. The headquarters of the Howard League for Prison Reform, named after the eighteenth-century investigator and reformer, are in a building directly opposite the church.

To the north, an early Southwark site of the gallows was at St Thomas Waterings, at the junction of Old Kent Road and Albany Road. This spot has special significance as the place where many Catholic martyrs, including St John Jones, were executed. Since their rejection of the reformed Church was held to be treason, most suffered the penalty for treason, and were hanged, drawn and quartered.

FURTHER READING

Material for this book has been gleaned from such a wide range of sources that a conventional bibliography might confuse rather than assist a reader who wanted to pursue the themes of this book. Instead, I offer a much shorter list of books which provide greater detail about either prisons or the London life in which they played a part.

Every historian of the subject relies greatly upon *The Criminal Prisons of London*, by Henry Mayhew and John Binny, first published in 1862 but happily reprinted by Frank Cass in 1971. This is a very detailed account (more than 600 pages) of the authors' researches into Victorian prison conditions, with enormous historical, statistical and anecdotal coverage. *Victorian Prison Lives*, by Philip Priestley (Methuen, 1985), uses prisoners' own words very effectively.

A wider history of the use of prison is given in *Imprisonment in England and Wales*, by Harding, Hines, Ireland and Rawlings (Croom Helm, 1985), while Seán McConville is producing the authoritative account of prison policy and management in his *History of English Prison Administration*; the first volume covering 1750–1877 appeared in 1981 (Routledge and Kegan Paul), and I am among those eager to read its successor.

Very thorough and very readable is *The Triple Tree*, by Donald Rumbelow, which tells the interlinked stories of Newgate, Tyburn and the Old Bailey (Harrap, 1982).

Executioner: Pierrepoint, by Albert Pierrepoint (Coronet), provides an odd but very informative and honest account of capital punishment from the point of view of a twentieth-century hangman.

On London, the essential source is as always Weireb and Hibbert's *The London Encyclopaedia* (Macmillan) – a magnificent work. For a chattier account, read the *Old London* reprints of the Alderman Press: Walter Thornbury's collection of history and anecdotes. Even chattier is the Everyman edition (Dent, 1987) of John Stow's *The Survey of London*, first published in 1598, and still one of the most valuable and readable sources of London history.

INDEX

Index

Index

Index

Index

Index

Index

Index

Index